Drama Lessons for Five to Eleven-Year-Olds

Judith Ackroyd and Jo Boulton

David Fulton Publishers
London

David Fulton Publishers Ltd
Ormond House, 26–27 Boswell Street, London WC1N 3JZ

www.fultonpublishers.co.uk

First published in Great Britain by David Fulton Publishers 2001

British Library Cataloguing in Publication Data
A catalogue record for this book is available from the British Library

ISBN 1–85346–739–1

The publishers would like to thank Yvonne Messenger for copy-editing and Sophie Cox for proofreading this book.

Typeset by Elite Typesetting Techniques, Eastleigh, Hampshire
Printed in Great Britain by The Cromwell Press Ltd, Trowbridge, Wilts.

Contents

Acknowledgements

We would like to thank the many school teachers in Northamptonshire who have experimented with these lessons. Special thanks for support in the preparation of this book are due to Richard Hardy, Athene Frisby, Angie Mathews, and to Puck Pilkington for reading and checking the typescript for us.

The birth of this book began many years ago when we worked with Tony Drane, then Inspector for English and Drama in the Northamptonshire Inspection and Advisory Service (NIAS). We are grateful for his support and friendship.

Thanks also to the friends who have shaped our practice and shared ideas over the years: Jonothan Neelands, Jane Tucker, Mal Gyte, Guy Dickens, Neil Kitson, Ian Spiby, Paul Bunyan, Jan Marshall and John Miller.

We would like to acknowledge Nelson Thornes for permission to reproduce an extract from *The Terrible Fate of Humpty Dumpty* by David Calcutt. Also Cambridge University Library for Nina de Garis Davies' *Ancient Egyptian Paintings*.

Dedication

With our love to the Andys

Introduction

This book is written in response to the interest of Northamptonshire teachers and students who have attended drama courses and wanted more materials. We have chosen to concentrate purely on drama lesson plans because there are already many excellent publications on topics such as theoretical underpinning, approaches to planning, lesson analyses and rationales for drama. A selection of these publications is listed at the back of this book. Some of the lessons in this book have been available as 'in house' materials in Northamptonshire, known as the 'Do Drama' books. We have chosen the favourites from these and have also included many new dramas. All of the dramas in this book are designed to fulfil learning objectives in various curriculum areas and develop particular skills. These are identified before each lesson guide. Many of these learning objectives relate directly to the National Curriculum for England and Wales. Since September 2000, the place of drama in the National Curriculum for English has been both cemented and extended. Children across the primary age phase have an entitlement to a wide range of drama experiences.

We are writing primarily for those teachers who have had little or no experience of teaching drama, but who have an interest in the subject, and a willingness to have a go at lessons devised, tried and tested by other teachers. Experienced teachers may appreciate some new materials to add to their repertoire. Each lesson therefore, provides all the information necessary for teachers to pick up and teach. Dramatic approaches are explained as they are employed and a list of the terms used in the lesson plans is included for those who wish to study and use some of the drama approaches in their own planning. The resources required are detailed and estimated times for each activity are given. These times cannot be exact because different children respond differently to the same stimuli and therefore an activity can take as much as thirty minutes more with one group than another. We have indicated where variance is most likely to occur.

The lesson plans are similar to play scripts in that the teacher, like the director, can manipulate, reshape, and even recontextualise them to create fresh new performance texts. A less experienced teacher or director may choose to remain closer to the scripted text. While the activities making up the dramatic scripts in this book are tightly structured, the overall possibilities for teaching the dramas are very flexible. Each drama is made up of a sequence of activities, most of which need to be followed in the order given. We are aware that teachers are working in different spaces with different children and with different constraints. The book is therefore designed so that teachers can do as much or as little of the drama at any one time as is appropriate. Sometimes teachers may choose to include fifteen minutes of drama activity over a series of literacy hours, and others may choose to teach a whole drama during a half-day session. Extension and additional suggestions for work that can be developed from the dramas are detailed within the drama plans. These suggestions include written, research, mathematical, and art possibilities. The Sun Wizard is laid out differently from the other lesson plans and appears first. This is to demonstrate how it is possible to teach one drama over an extended six-week period in regular sessions of half an hour. Many of the other dramas could be taught in the same way over a long period.

Teaching drama has given us enormous pleasure and we are excited by its possibilities to enhance children's learning experiences. We hope that you will also become 'hooked'.

Notes for using this book

1. It is essential to read the lesson plan all the way through before starting.

2. All the teacher roles can be male or female. You can change the names as appropriate. For clarity and continuity, we have referred to the teacher as 'she' throughout the text. Similarly, when speaking about an individual child we have adopted the term 'he'.

3. The plans can be adapted if you feel that you would like to give more time to some activities or place more emphasis on some of the sections.

4. The sections in italic san-serif fonts indicate words that are spoken by the teacher or examples of questions and responses from children.

5. The suggested age range for each lesson is fairly wide. This is deliberate. The content is appropriate for the whole age range suggested in the plan and advice is given to help the teacher to differentiate questions and to support or extend the children as necessary.

6. Once you have used some of the dramatic activities through teaching the lessons provided you may wish to select some from the list which follows (Terms used in the lesson plans) to use in your own planning.

7. The list of recommended reading includes books offering theoretical introductions to using drama in the primary school, further lesson plans, and examples of different dramatic approaches that will be helpful in your planning.

Terms used in the lesson plans

Collective drawing

Individuals add detail to a picture or map. Children come forward one or two at a time and draw on to the basic outline, which has been prepared by the teacher. Sometimes it will be quicker to give each child a piece of paper or a 'Post-it' note on which to draw. These individual drawings can then be stuck onto the outline picture. This way of working gives the finished product collective ownership. If time is restricted, the picture can be finished later.

Collective or collaborative storytelling

The whole class joins in with the telling of the story. The teacher leads the telling and invites individuals to supply words, sound effects, phrases or whole sentences. This way the detail is supplied by the children while the development of the plot is controlled by the teacher.

Costuming

Selected props or items of clothing are chosen by the teacher to indicate a particular role to the class. It is important that any costume is put on in front of the children so they observe the teacher going into role in front of them, and there is no confusion about who the teacher actually is. Sometimes with younger children you can let the children help you to put on the items of clothing, helping with fastenings and giving advice as to which to put on first.

Defining space

This is the way in which the teacher and class agree on the parameters and features of the fictional space. In the process the classroom space is defined as the place in the drama. Items of furniture may be used to define the space. Two chairs, for example, may mark the position of the gateposts leading to the castle.

Hot seating

The teacher or the child is questioned in role by the others. Whoever is on the 'hot seat' answers as their character would.

Improvisation

The children act and speak in role. There is no pre-planning. Improvisation is often led by the teacher in role enabling her to keep control of the direction of the improvisation.

Narration

Teacher narration in drama activities is often a very useful controlling device! The teacher is empowered to dictate particular aspects of the drama. A class working noisily, for example, may hear the teacher narrate, 'Gradually they fell silent. The travellers were too tired to speak.' Narration can also be used to excite or build tension in the drama.

'Not one of the travellers had ever seen what lay behind the tall grey wall. Many had guessed, but no one was sure.'

Overheard conversations

Children in groups make up conversations that people in their drama may have had. They then overhear one another's conversations as though they are eavesdropping. This enables the children to work in small groups and gives all of them the chance to comment in role on the action of the drama.

Ritual

Any action, no matter how simple and mundane, can be performed in a formal and dignified manner to make the actions seem significant. Putting goodies into Grandma's basket in a ritualistic manner (one at a time with a particular phrase or gesture) will bring about a more serious level of thought and an exciting atmosphere.

Role on the wall

The outline of a person is drawn onto a large sheet of paper. Information about the person in the drama is collected and written around the outline. It is possible to contrast different types of information in a role on the wall. What the character says can be written in one colour and what she thinks in another.

Sculpting

This way of working involves children making statues of each other or the teacher through suggestions and physical manipulation. Sculptures can be made to crystallise ideas about a character, such as what the bully looked like; or to express a feeling, such as how anger could be physically represented.

Statementing

Statementing involves the children literally in making statements about a person, event or place in the drama. The statements can be made in a ritualistic manner, with children stepping forward one at a time to say their statement. They may remain frozen in a gesture appropriate to the statement.

Still image or frozen picture

These are similar to sculpting but involve small groups or the whole class. Using their own bodies, children depict a moment in time. It is literally a frozen moment when we imagine time has stopped, giving us the opportunity to look more closely at it.

Teacher in role

The teacher takes the role of a character in the drama. This enables the teacher to work with the children from inside the drama. Additional information can be given through the teacher's role and questions asked to challenge the children's ideas.

Thought tracking: thought tunnels and thought tapping

Thought tracking enables children in role to speak aloud the thoughts that would normally remain concealed. This can be done in different ways such as 'thought tunnels' and 'thought tapping'.

Thought tunnels require the children to face one another in two lines. The teacher or a child walks slowly between the two lines, through the tunnel, in role as character X in the drama. The thought tunnel can vary depending on what you want to explore. You may wish to consider the thoughts of character X by asking the children to speak aloud the thoughts that character X might have at this point in the drama. It is best to have voices from alternating sides speaking at the moment character X passes them by. Alternatively, you may wish to consider the thoughts that other people have about character X, asking children to provide these as character X walks by.

Thought tapping is when the teacher literally taps a child on the shoulder as a signal for the child to speak the thoughts of the character he is playing. This may be done in the midst of mimed activity or in still images.

Chapter 1

The Sun Wizard
Light and dark

The people of a small village are preparing for a very important event that is to take place in the evening when it is dark. However, on the evening of the event darkness refuses to fall for the first time ever. The surprised villagers receive a letter from the Sun Wizard. He tells them that he has cast a special spell preventing the sun from ever setting again. What can the villagers do to solve the problem? Together they confront the wizard who turns out to be afraid of the dark, especially the noises he hears when he is in bed. Can the villagers persuade him to change his mind and see that the dark is not really frightening when you know what is making the noises?

Age group	5–8 years
Curriculum area focus	**Science** Plants need light to grow. Identifying different light sources, including the sun. Darkness is the absence of light.
Speaking and listening	Gaining and maintaining the interest and response of different audiences. Asking relevant questions to clarify and extend ideas. Making contributions relevant to the topic. Creating, adapting and sustaining different roles. Using dramatic techniques to explore characters and issues.
PSHE and Citizenship	Recognising and dealing with feelings positively. Caring for others. Considering social dilemmas.

Resources	Letter or scroll from the Sun Wizard (see Figure 1.2, p. 8). Large paper or whiteboard and pens. Outline map (see Figure 1.3, p. 10). Cloak or prop for the wizard.
Time	Six sessions of approximately 30 minutes. This drama is also easily adapted for longer sessions of one hour or shorter sessions of about 15 minutes each.

Notes

1. This drama is particularly appropriate to link with a science topic looking at day and night or light and dark.
2. As with many of our dramas written for younger children, the story takes place in a village. This doesn't have to be the setting but it gives the feeling of a traditional story to the drama, which also contains other familiar story elements such as wizards and spells.
3. This is a drama that is suitable to be used with very young children. It draws very much on imaginative play experiences but at the same time concentrates on teaching particular drama skills that may not have been used before, such as mime, still images, whole group improvisation.
4. It could be useful to start introducing some of the ideas about light and dark in a science lesson that takes place before the drama. This is not crucial but will save time during the drama session.

Drama activities
Session 1
(30 minutes)

1. What do we know about day and night?

[Discussion]
Tell the children that the story they are going to tell is about day and night. Ask the children to think about things that take place at night and things that happen during the day when it is light. These things can be brainstormed onto a large sheet of paper divided in to two columns (see Figure 1.1). Alternatively the children could be given pictures of daytime and night activities to sort into the two sets.

Figure 1.1   An example brainstorm of things that happen during the day and at night

2. Miming things that happen in the day and things that happen at night

[Mime]
Take one or two examples of daytime activities that are done by people, suggested by the children and mime the activities as a whole group. Examples are: waking up in the morning, walking to school, playing football, flying a kite, hanging out the washing, shopping.

Encourage the children to think carefully about the mime, their movements, and also gesture and facial expression.

How do we walk to school? Are we happy skipping along like this?

Demonstrate and encourage all of the children to copy you.

Sometimes we might drag our heels like this.

Again, encourage the children to copy your mime.

Now you show me how you walk to school/the park.

Emphasise that miming doesn't involve speaking and, although this is difficult to achieve, keep reminding them about the need for silence.

The children choose a way they prefer and mime their walk.

3. Making pictures of things that happen in the day and at night

[Still image and talking to the image]
Introduce the 'freeze' control. Ask the children to do their mimes and then stop on the instruction '1-2-3 freeze!' Tell them that this looks

like a picture that could come from a storybook. The special thing is that with this picture you are able to speak to the people in the picture by touching them one at a time on the shoulder. Demonstrate this with a few children asking questions appropriate to their position. Questions should be differentiated according to the children's confidence and ability. The first and the last questions on this list demand different levels of response.

> *What are you doing on this lovely day?*
>
> *What clothes are you putting on?*
>
> *Where are you standing?*
>
> *Are you on your own or are you fishing with your friends?*
>
> *How long does it take you to walk to school?*
>
> *Why are you looking so gloomy?*
>
> *Is it a sunny day?*
>
> *What will you do in the park?*
>
> *Can you see anyone else on the beach?*
>
> *I can see you are holding something. Can you tell me what it is?*
>
> *What does the sand feel like under your feet?*

Another special thing is that when you clap the picture comes to life again and the mimes can continue.

Now choose a couple of night activities to mime and encourage the children to join in as before. Examples are: watching fireworks, holding sparklers, looking at the stars and the moon, getting ready for bed.

These night mimes can again be frozen into still pictures and individuals questioned as before.

4. Bringing the pictures to life

[Improvisation]
Tell the children that this time they will be able to talk when they are doing their activities. They can talk to one another or to themselves. (Most begin by making noises and not interacting with others, but this is fine.)

Choose either the day or night activities to explore in this way.

Start off with each child miming a chosen activity and then give an instruction for it to move into improvised conversations. After a few seconds use the freeze control to stop the movement and freeze in a still image.

Additional activities

- Individuals or groups can make lists of things that happen in the day and at night.
- Collect and sort pictures of day and night.
- Do paintings/collage of day and night scenes.
- Collect and read day and night stories and poems.
- Look at non-fiction books about day and night. Add to the lists some more unusual things that happen.
- Find out about why we have day and night.

1. Warm up – revising mime and still image

*Session 2
(30 minutes)*

[Mime or improvisation]
Remind the children of the work completed in the previous session. Perhaps recap with a couple of mimed activities and maybe introduce a couple of new mimes. Also remind them of improvisation and the freeze control.

2. Setting the scene

[Mime, still image with thought tap and narration]
Tell the children that you are going to start to tell the story and that they are going to help you by being the people in the story. Tell them to choose one of the day activities to mime and after a few seconds freeze the picture as they did earlier. Narrate the following:

Once, in a place very far from here there was a little village. In the village there lived all kinds of different people. If you walked through the village on a sunny day you would be sure to see the villagers out and about doing lots of different things.

Talk to the children about the things they are doing in the village today.

Where are you in the village today?

What are you doing?

What are you carrying in your heavy bag?

What is your dog called?

Can you tell me what buildings you can see around you?

Do you live near the market place?

What are you planting in your garden?

Are you on your way to the shop? What will you buy?

Indicate that the image can come to life when you clap your hands. Leave the mime to run for a few seconds and then freeze it again.

Now tell the children that they are now going to do their chosen night mime. Start them off and then after a few seconds give the freeze command and narrate the following:

The people all loved to be out in the sunshine during the day but also loved the evening time. It was then that they could do all the things that they enjoyed doing when it was dark. Some of them liked to…

Touch a few individuals on the shoulder and ask them to say what they enjoy doing in the dark.

Additional activities

- Build up belief about the village.
  - Individual children can decide on a character for themselves in the village.
  - They draw pictures of their own characters.
  - They possibly write something about their own character.
  - Draw a map of the village.
  - Draw a picture of houses and people in the village.
  - Indicate where the owl's nest and badger's set are.
  - Label the village pond, wood, road, church.
  - Give the village a name.
- Find out about light sources – natural and man-made.
- Find out information about the sun, the moon and stars.

Session 3 (30 minutes)

You have to make certain decisions in this session about the choice of event that is the focus of the session. Decide on a special event that is going to take place in the village. You could ask the children to suggest what could be happening. This event can only happen in the dark. You could take on a more authoritative role such as the village elder.

1. Meeting the villagers

[Children in role]
Hopefully the children will have had the opportunity to think about the person that they are going to be in the story before this session starts. If not, ask them to decide now. Ask all the villagers to introduce themselves to the rest of the group.

2. The Village Celebration is prepared

[Narration and brainstorm]

> *The people of the village were very excited. They were getting ready*
> *for a special bonfire party/ switching on the Christmas lights/*
> *summer barbecue that was going to take place that very evening.*
> *Everyone had a special job to do to get the party ready.*

Ask the children what kind of things the people would have to do to prepare for the party. Brainstorm a list, for example:
making food
putting up decorations
building the bonfire
organising music.

Depending on the age and experience of the children, select one of the following ways of improvising the scene:

(a) Ask the children to choose something to do to help get the party ready and improvise the scene. Ask them to tell you what it is they have chosen to do. In this improvisation you will go round chatting and giving advice about what needs doing:

> *Now have you got everything you need?*

> *Will we have enough sandwiches?*

> *Who is in charge of the fairy lights?*

> *Did anyone buy any sparklers?*

> *Can someone help me with this table?*

(b) Lead the children in improvising with everyone making food or putting up decorations together:

> *Let's start with putting up the fairy lights. Everyone get some out of*
> *this box. Be careful with them because they're very delicate. Stretch*
> *up like this and hang them on the hooks like this. I'll just turn them*
> *on to test that they're working. That looks brilliant. I'll turn them off*
> *until it gets dark. We need it to be dark so that we can see the*
> *lights in all their glory. What's next? Oh yes, the food…*

Additional activities

- Draw pictures or write about jobs done to prepare the party.
- Design posters advertising the event.

Session 4
(30 minutes)

1. Night doesn't fall

[Narration, letter, discussion and map making]
Before the session starts, hide the scroll or the envelope containing the letter from the Sun Wizard (see Figure 1.2) in a strategic place to be retrieved at the appropriate moment.

Ask the children to remember where they were standing in the village and take up positions again. Start with a brief recap of the story so far ending with:

After a great deal of hard work the party was ready. Everyone changed into their best clothes and sat down to wait for it to get dark so that the party could begin. They waited and waited and waited but the sun stayed high in the sky. It was getting very late but still the sun did not go down and the sky was still blue and very bright. Whatever could have happened?

Gather the children and sit down on the floor.

I wonder what has happened?

Has anyone got any ideas?

Invite some speculation but cut this short by announcing:

I just saw a messenger quietly creep up and drop something over there. It seems to be a message of some kind.

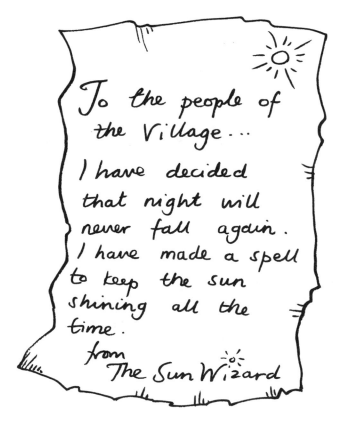

Figure 1.2 The letter from the Sun Wizard

2. A letter arrives

Pick up the scroll or envelope from the hiding place (see Figure 1.2). Read the letter or invite someone to help with the reading. It says that the sun will not set again because he has cast a spell to prevent it.

> *What will we do if it never gets dark again?*
>
> *What things will not be able to happen?*
>
> *What can be done about this problem?*
>
> *Has anyone ever heard about this Sun Wizard before?*
>
> *Where does he live? Is there an address on the letter?*

If the children do not suggest it then you will need to say:

> *Should we try to talk to him and see if we can find out why he's cast this spell?*
>
> *What will we say to the wizard?*
>
> *How will we persuade him to change the spell?*
>
> *What will happen if he won't talk to us? Perhaps we should write a letter to take with us and then if he won't see us we can put it through the letterbox.*

Additional activities

- Use a large piece or number of pieces of paper stuck together with an outline map suggested (see Figure 1.3). Encourage the children to draw features onto the map – stream, trees, hills, roads, etc.
- Draw pictures of what they think the wizard's house might look like.
- Write a letter to the wizard giving reasons for him to change his spell (shared or individual writing).
- Draw pictures and write words to predict what the wizard will look like.

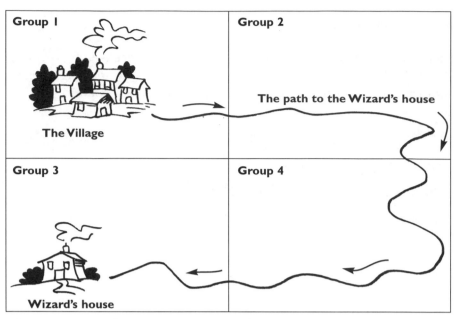

Figure 1.3 Outline map to prepare for journey

Session 5 (30 minutes)

1. What do we know about the Sun Wizard?

[Discussion]

In this session the children will meet the teacher in role as the Sun Wizard. Introduce this idea to the children at the beginning of the session. Agree signals for when you are in and out of role.

If you are using a cloak to wear when you are the wizard, show it to the children.

When I put on this cloak I will be the Sun Wizard

or

When I walk over to the door and back again I will be the Sun Wizard.

Lead a discussion about the wizard:

Can you remember what kind of house you think the wizard lives in?

What do you think the wizard might be like when we meet him?

What will we say when we first meet him?

Let's read our letter(s) (if these were done as an additional activity).

2. The journey to the wizard's house

[Improvisation]

Now, have we got the map? Which way do we go?

Lead the children around the room imagining the journey and describing the features as you go. It works well if you can lead the children out of the class and across the playground or through the hall. This makes the journey even more exciting and memorable.

Be careful of this tree-trunk, pick your feet up high.

Watch out for the snake pit. Jump over the stream.

When you feel the journey has been completed, stop the children and gather the children together.

We've arrived outside the wizard's house. What can you see?

Ask individuals to describe what they can see. Encourage description of sun-colours, lights blazing.

3. Meeting the Sun Wizard

[Teacher in role and meeting]
Tell the children that in the next part of the story you are going to be the wizard. You will be in your house. Agree how he will know that the villagers have arrived. Will they knock?

On the agreed signal greet the villagers. The wizard is very nervous and jumpy. Make sure you give enough time for the children to respond to you.

Hello everyone. Who are you?

I don't get many visitors. Welcome to my home. Would you like to come in? Please sit down.

What is it you wanted?

Oh yes, the spell. Well I'm sorry but you won't make me change my mind. There is no way I am going to let it get dark again.

Through comments and questions, enable the villagers to tell the wizard about the celebration they have planned. Also invite them to tell you about the other things that only happen at night through questions such as:

Why is night so important anyway?

But surely all of these things can happen in the light, and the badgers and foxes will soon get used to waking up in the light, won't they?

I hate the dark. I just can't take any more.

Let the villagers question the wizard. Don't give too much information away at once. Eventually, tell the villagers that there are too many horrible frightening things at night. You haven't been able to sleep properly for weeks with a 'Twit Twoooo' noise outside. Then there is the tapping on the bedroom window, the one on the forest side of your bedroom. You can't see in the dark and it's frightening.

Eventually let the villagers persuade you that the noises are all easily explained and it will be a disaster for so many animals, plants and people if it never gets dark again.

Finish the session by saying:

Well, I suppose you're right. I'm just being silly really. I know that it's only an owl sitting on the tree outside my window and hooting and I know that the branch scratches my window when the wind blows. Thank you for explaining all these things to me. And you're right about all of the animals too.

I'll have to make a new spell to change things again. I think I'll need your help for this special spell. I would like you all to think of a special word to say to make the spell work. It should be a long and interesting word that sounds exciting. Do you think you can all find a word like that? It doesn't have to be a magic word like 'abracadabra' but one that sounds good like 'supersonic' or 'fabulous'. These kinds of words have a lot of magic power.

Take off the cloak and indicate that the meeting with the wizard is over for today.

4. What did we find out about the wizard?

[Discussion]
Out of role, discuss the wizard and his problems. Is there anything else the children could suggest to make him feel better?

Additional activities

- Draw pictures of the meeting with the wizard.
- Add speech bubbles or thought bubbles to the characters.
- Decide on the special word to use in the spell. Write the word.

*Session 6
(30 minutes)*

1. The spell and the celebration

[Teacher in role and narration]
In this final session the children help the wizard to make a spell and invite him to join them in their celebration. Remind the children that the story will continue from where it was left last time – on the evening planned for the village celebration.

Ask the children to stand in a circle.

Teacher in role as the Sun Wizard says:

Thank you all so much for coming to see me this evening. You've really helped me to see how silly I've been. Now let's see if we can work together and make a reversing spell. Have you all thought of a word? Good.

Invite the villagers one at a time to say their word. Write the word on to a 'Post-it' and stick it onto a large sheet of paper.
Tell the children to close their eyes. Count to three. Clap.

Open your eyes everyone. The spell's worked! Well done. I can feel that the sun is beginning to go down and you will be able to have your party. Don't let me hold you up.

Hopefully the villagers will invite the wizard. He will need a little persuading but will be happy to go. If session time allows, improvise the party. Alternatively, finish the session with narration:

The people of the village had a wonderful party and the wizard enjoyed himself very much. He was still rather worried about sleeping in the dark but his new friends told him again not to be afraid and to leave the light on for the time being if he was feeling a little scared. And that is the end of our story about the villagers and the Sun Wizard.

Ask the children to stand in a circle. Ask the children to come forward one at a time to say something about the wizard. Examples can be given by the teacher to give the children ideas:

I liked the wizard.

He was sad and we helped him.

He was frightened of the dark.

He made a spell.

2. Reflection

[Discussion]
Discuss the story. Recap on the reasons for the wizard's fear of the dark and discuss the explanations given by the villagers.
Perhaps go on to discuss the children's own fears if appropriate.

Are there times when you have been scared of something?

What did you do?

Chapter 2

The Sad Clown
Helping others

The children meet a very miserable clown who is in need of their help. The clown has always wanted to work in the circus but is in danger of being thrown out because he can't make the audience laugh. The children teach the clown how to be funny.

Age group	5–8 years
Curriculum area focus	**English (S&L) PSHE and Citizenship**
Speaking and listening	Making plans and investigating. Sharing ideas and experiences. Commenting and reporting. Working in role. Speaking to different people, varying speech to different circumstances. Taking account of listeners. Persuading, explaining, questioning.
PSHE and Citizenship	Keeping safe. Problem solving. Helping and caring for others. Working together.
Resources	Books about or pictures of the circus. Props and/or costume for clown – red nose, hat, juggling balls or oranges, large hanky. Optional face paints. A full clown costume is a bonus. Large, oversized and colourful bag containing props.
Time	This session can take between 30 minutes and one hour.

1. This drama is ideal for younger children and/or those inexperienced in drama because it engages the children as one group throughout. The teacher maintains close control of the unfolding dramatic fiction in which the children can contribute their own ideas.

2. This is potentially a fairly physical drama session for the teacher, depending on which tricks the children suggest that you do. It may be worth laying down some ground rules when you first go in to role as the clown, saying that you have a bad back that will prevent you from doing anything too adventurous. Otherwise, be prepared to do forward rolls and stand on your head – the children always think that is very funny!

3. The use of props and/or costume for this drama is extremely beneficial. It is really worth trying to beg or borrow a clown costume, otherwise a red nose, pointed hat or a set of juggling balls will do.

1. What do we know about the circus? (5 minutes)

[Discussion]
Introduce the story by leading a general discussion about circuses. This may need to be done using a picture or even a storybook with which the children may be familiar.

Has anyone ever been to a circus or seen one on television?

What happens at the circus?

What kinds of acts could you see?

Who is in charge at the circus?

What does the ringmaster usually wear to look smart and important?

What do the clowns do?

Do clowns wear any special clothes?

Tell the children that they are going to tell a story about a circus in their drama today. Tell them that there is going to be a special person in the story that they are going to meet and this person is the owner of the bag.

2. What is in the bag? Looking at the clown's costume (5 minutes)

[Discussion]
Place the bag of clothes or clown props in the centre of the circle of children. Invite children one at a time to take something out of the bag. Comment on each item:

What do you think this is?

What kind of person would need/wear this?

What do you think the balls/oranges are for?

This is a strange hat! Who would wear one like this?

Lay the items out on the floor for everyone to see.

3. Putting on the costume (5 minutes)

[Costuming]
Tell the children that in the story you are going to be the clown who owns these things, and that you are going to wear the costume or have these things (hat, juggling balls, red nose). You may need help with dressing or deciding how to hold things correctly so you could invite the children to help you dress. Alternatively, they can suggest the order for putting on the clothes. As you are being dressed, it is important to keep up a commentary about what is happening and you can ask more questions to gather the children's collective knowledge about clowns and circuses. If you are feeling confident or are working with a small group of children, you may invite them to paint your face to make you look like a clown.

Has anyone ever seen a clown?

What do clowns do?

How do they make people laugh?

Is it a man or a lady clown?

What do you think is a good name for a clown?

Take a few suggestions of names and choose one for the clown whom the children are going to meet.

Now that you are dressed as the clown or are holding the clown's props, tell the children that they are going to be able to speak to the clown in a couple of minutes. How do they expect the clown to behave? Happy? Jumping about? Tell the children that the clown will come and talk to them now. Walk away from the children and return in role as the clown.

4. Meeting the sad clown (10–20 minutes)

[Teacher in role as the clown, and giving advice]
Clown enters with a very sad face. Pulls out a large hanky, blows nose loudly and sighs.

Oh dear, whatever shall I do? I'm so miserable.

Hopefully the children will ask what is wrong. If they don't (which is very unlikely), you could add:

No one seems to care about me.

And if necessary:

I suppose you are not interested in me either, are you?

The clown tells the children:

I've wanted to be a clown all my life. I used to go to the circus and laugh at the clowns and wish that I could be one. Then the other day I was walking past this circus tent when the ringmaster ran out asking if anyone could help him. The clown had got the chicken pox and couldn't go on that night. I knew that was my chance to be a clown and I told the ringmaster that I could do it. So, he gave me a job! But I wasn't any good at all. No one laughed at me. The ringmaster said I was useless and if I wasn't any better tonight then I would have to leave. I don't want to leave. I love working here. I didn't think that I was too bad really. What can I do?

The children will probably ask you what things you did, but if not you can ask them:

Shall I show you what I did?

Then give an example of a pathetic joke with a slow delivery, a miserable face and a useless attempt at acrobatics or juggling!

Can the children suggest how the clown's act can be improved and suggest some exciting things to put into it for the show tonight? Invite individual children to demonstrate their suggestion and try to copy them, badly at first then improving. Suggestions should come freely from the children but a few possibilities may include:

- introducing the show in a loud voice
- big gestures
- telling funny jokes with a smile
- falling over or rolling
- juggling with the balls or oranges (you don't have to be successful, but will assure the children you will practise)
- throwing buckets of pretend water
- funny walks
- balancing on one leg and toppling over in a hilarious way.

As the children make more suggestions and you try things out you can grow in confidence.

Do you think I'm getting better?

Should I do it like this or would it look better like this?

How should my face look?

Would it be a good idea to make these things in to a little show?

Perhaps we could write a list of the things that I am going to do in the right order so I don't forget.

5. Making a list and rehearsing the show (5 minutes)

[Demonstration and rehearsal]
The clown asks the children to decide in which order to perform the stunts. The order can be written down or remembered, whichever is appropriate. Perform the show in the right order asking the children to prompt you. Usually there is spontaneous applause! Ask the children to suggest if there are any improvements. Take their advice. Tell the children it is time for your show now and thank them for their help. Leave waving merrily and take off the costume.

6. How did the story end? (5 minutes)

[Narration]
Finish the story by asking the children what they think happened that night. Use their ideas to narrate a satisfactory ending such as:

The clown was an enormous success that night. The ringmaster couldn't believe his eyes. The crowd laughed and clapped so loudly you could hear the noise miles away. The ringmaster thanked the clown for a splendid performance and offered him a permanent job in the circus.

The clown worked happily there for many years and always remembered the day that his friends, the children, showed him how to be a proper funny clown.

7. Reflection (5 minutes)

Discuss the story. Was the clown as they had expected? How had they helped the clown?

Additional possibilities

1. Writing activities
   These activities can be undertaken individually, in pairs, groups or as whole class shared writing:
   (a) Writing a list of the clown's routine.
   (b) Storyboarding the routine. Ask the children to draw a series of pictures to illustrate the clown's routine with the main verb written below. For example: juggling.
   (c) Creating speech bubbles for the clown and the ringmaster.
   (d) Composing newspaper headlines.
   (e) Writing a programme entry for the new clown.
   (f) Designing a poster advertising the circus.

2. Other activities
   (a) Set up an imaginative play area as the circus ring.
   (b) Draw or paint pictures of the clown and the ringmaster.
   (c) Children perform their own clown show.
   (d) Design clown make-up.

Chapter 3

Suzie and the Snow
Safety

Suzie is sad and won't go out to play in the snow. The children try to find out why and gradually learn about Suzie's accident on the ice last year. The past is brought to life with the children all taking part in it. Finally, they advise her about how she can play out in the snow safely.

Age group	5–8 years
Curriculum area focus	**Citizenship**
Speaking and listening	Choosing words with precision. Taking into account the needs of listeners. Sustaining concentration. Asking questions to clarify understanding. Remembering specific points. Taking turns in speaking. Extending ideas in the light of discussion. Using language and actions to explore and convey situations, characters and emotions. Creating and sustaining roles.
PSHE and Citizenship	Keeping safe, preparing to play an active role as citizens. Listening to people, and playing and working cooperatively. Family and friends should care for each other.
Resources	Suzie's diary entry is provided (see Figure 3.1). A jacket (activity 5).

Time	Approximately two hours, or longer if the work is videoed in activity 8.

Notes

1. The teacher is required to take the role of Suzie in this drama. It involves whole class drama for the most part.
2. The range of different types of talk is extensive. The children have to be very selective in interaction with Suzie, who is at one moment shy and nervous, a show off at another, and, finally, embarrassed and frightened. If they do not approach Suzie appropriately, they will not discover what happened.
3. There is also a wide range of types of dramatic activity and the room will need to be cleared for many of them.
4. The children are given the rare opportunity of speaking to the teacher in role as a child who is more vulnerable than they are and who needs their advice. This is clearly a role reversal of the children's usual experience when they are the vulnerable ones. Teachers find this a wonderful experience on both sides. It does not require a strong 'performance' as a child. You don't need to be childish, but use a few simple gestures or signs, such as tugging at your sleeve. Other suggestions are given below.

Drama activities

1. What is the matter with Suzie? (10 minutes)

[Listening, discussion and prediction]
Sit in a circle on chairs. Explain that you will be doing a drama about an imaginary person called Suzie who is about the same age as the children. You will pretend to have a page from her diary (see Figure 3.1).

What is a diary?

Why might some diaries be secret?

Who uses diaries?

What is put into diaries?

Ask the class to listen to the diary and try to work out what is going on. Read the diary provided. Discuss.

Which single words would describe how she feels?

Why is she feeling like this, do you think?

Why doesn't she like the snow?

What might have happened?

What could her Dad have meant by saying she could play sensibly?

FEBRUARY 16th

I heard the weather on the television. It said there may be snow. I wish it could be summer. Oh, please don't let it snow. All my friends will be out. They'll be knocking on the door. They wont understand why I wont go out with them. My Dad says I'm silly and that I could play out sensibly, though I know he stills feels afraid about what happened. My sister doesn't like being out in the snow much now either.

The weather man does get it wrong sometimes, Dad says he does. Maybe he was wrong this time.

© Ackroyd, J. and Boulton, J. (2001) *Drama Lessons for Five to Eleven-Year-Olds*. London: David Fulton Publishers. www.fultonpublishers.co.uk

Figure 3.1 Suzie's diary (This could be photocopied and enlarged for use with the class)

2. Meeting Suzie (15 minutes)

[Teacher in role, whole class meeting]
Invite the class to meet Suzie to try to find out what has happened.

What should they ask?

How should they speak to someone who is upset?

What should they begin with saying?

How will they ensure Suzie knows that she can trust them?

What sort of voices and expression should they use?

What does a 'kind' voice (or any other suggestion) sound like?

Teacher leaves the circle and returns as Suzie. She is very, very shy and hardly dares to look at the children. She hesitates before sitting in the circle, or may even wait to be invited to sit down. Suzie could have a mannerism to depict her shyness, such as tugging on her sleeve or swinging her legs or wrapping them around the chair leg.

Suzie does not give much information away and at first changes the subject if asked about snow! She talks about Lego cranes, boats and summer games... anything but snow and winter!

If the children do not press Suzie to talk, then entice questions by giving incomplete information, 'I don't like going out – not after what happened'. Eventually, she feels ready to tell the class:

> *It was a snowy Sunday...everyone was there in the park...fun, snowballs, sledging, scarves and woolly hats...I boasted about my ice skating...I said that I could skate up the river, round the three bends, through the wood to the bridge and back...they warned me...they all said I mustn't, said I was silly...I wish I'd listened...*

Suzie leaves the circle too upset to go on.

3. Last year in the park (15 minutes)

[Still image and thought tap]
Suggest that they all go back in time to find out what happened in the park. First, they need to create a big picture of the scene at the park that day. Everyone will become a person in that scene who was there that day.

> *What do we know about the park that day?*

> *What were you doing? Whereabouts were you?*

Define and organise the space:

> *Where shall we imagine the river is?*

> *Where is the slope for the sledging?*

> *In which direction are the woods and the bridge that Suzie spoke of?*

Children move into the space and decide who they were with and what they were doing on that day, and freeze in a still image depicting their activity – for example, snowballing or building a snowman. Teacher admires the scene they have created and explains that she can move into this scene and bring people to life by touching their shoulders. A second tap on their shoulders freezes them again.

Tap individuals and ask about what they are doing, who they are throwing a snowball at, what the snow feels like in the fingers, what it feels like to sledge so quickly, what will be used for the snowman's eyes, and so on. A second tap freezes them into still silence again so that the scene remains fixed.

4. Suzie shows off (20 minutes)

[Teacher in role and improvisation]
Explain that you will take the role of Suzie. As you speak to the children they will come to life and respond. Check that they remember the sort of things that the other children had said to Suzie when she boasted about her skating idea. After you have spoken to them they become part of the still image again.

Suzie enters from one side and explains her idea to individuals and small groups of children. They will answer back, saying she is silly, or something similar. She moves on to try to persuade others to join her, calling them 'chickens' and 'cowards'. Once she has approached all the children she moves towards the edge of the area in the direction of the woods and bridge, and then turns around suddenly. Now narrate in an excited tone. (This can be read from the page if it is more comfortable for you. It doesn't spoil the effect, although just speaking the story is more fun.)

> *She skated up the river, got around the first two bends and was quickly in the wood. The air was crisp; the woods were quiet. Suddenly she felt a crack under her foot. She lurched forward in an attempt to keep her balance, but almost at once her right foot was through the ice.*
>
> *Scrambling, gasping, panicking, soon she was in the icy cold water up to her arm-pits, arms stretched out so she wouldn't go down completely. The shouting and screaming became frantic shrieking, but no one heard. She was too far away. She couldn't feel much of her body, it all felt numb and her hands were hardly recognisable, being a blend of red and blue. She wondered how long she could keep her position. Would anyone walk far enough into the wood to see or hear her?*

5. Suzie's thoughts (10 minutes)

[Thought tracking]
The children stand in a circle. Teacher moves into the middle and places a jacket on the floor, arranging it carefully in silence, positioning the arms outstretched either side.

Stepping back into the circle, ask the children to think about what Suzie will be thinking as she clings on to the ice. One at a time children take a step forward and say something that Suzie could have been thinking (see Figure 3.2).

Figure 3.2   Suzie's thoughts

6. Suzie's escape (10–30 minutes)

[Story circles or puppets]
We know that Suzie survived because we met her a year after the accident. How was she rescued? The possible stories of her rescue can be told in either of the following ways:

- [Story circle] Children work in the whole class group and take it in turns to tell a little bit of the story of her way out of the ice. By the time they get around the whole circle the story must finish. This means that they all need to consider how much or how little to tell when it is their turn. Story circles could also be carried out with small groups. Each group tells a story going around their circle a few times.

- [Puppets] In small groups, the story is made up and then told using puppets. Puppets need not be 'real' puppets, but anything that happens to be around. We have seen pencil cases used as rescuers, and plants as the crying Suzie. Each child manipulates a puppet and provides its voice, as well as some narration.

7. Persuading Suzie to play out (10 minutes)

[Teacher in role and whole class meeting]
Discuss the following questions with the children.

How can we help Suzie, who was very silly and is STILL afraid to go out in the snow?

Would we be able to explain that it can be safe to play out in the snow?

Do you think you could encourage her to go outside?

What would you say?

Shall I get Suzie?

The task is set: the children now try to advise Suzie that she could play out, enjoy herself and still be perfectly safe. Teacher in role as Suzie is reluctant at first, making the class work hard to convince her. Finally, when they convince her, she says she will go and get her Wellington boots.

8. Safety promotion videos (20 minutes minimum)

[Teacher in role; small group performance]
This activity will be appropriate for older children who can work on their own in groups. It will obviously take a few hours if the children's work is videoed.

Speak to the children as though they are film-makers. Tell them that, as a result of Suzie's accident, all school children are to be shown a video that warns children about the dangers of snow and moving about on ice, giving advice on safety. (You may prefer to choose a local hazardous environment such as gravel pits or mudflats.) It is crucial that the videos are fun and lively so that the children they are aimed at will enjoy them and take the message seriously.

In small groups the children plan and perform something that they think would be suitable for the video. They may include an interview with Suzie or a friend, they may make up a jingle, make a number of points to remember in an appropriate language register, or they may construct a re-enactment of the accident. In some schools it may be possible to video record the groups' work and show the videos to other classes, or in an assembly. Titles or captions can be made on large sheets of sugar paper or whiteboards and videoed with sound effects of words, noises or music.

Additional possibilities

1. Individual writing or shared writing task
   Children write additional entries in Suzie's diary, or as other children who were in the park.

2. Shared writing and drawing activity
   (a) A poster can be made to warn children of dangers.
   (b) A list of rules for safe behaviour could be constructed.

Chapter 4

The Baker's Shop
Health care

Mr Baker is a much loved and respected figure in the village, well known for his delicious bread and cakes. One day the children are disturbed to find that his shop window is empty. What could be the problem? The children are invited to help the injured baker make bread and cakes. They are also asked to help design and make a surprise birthday cake for the King. When they deliver the cake to the palace they find that the King has toothache because he has failed to take care of his teeth. The children teach him how to brush his teeth properly.

Age group	5–8 years
Curriculum area focus	**English (S&L)** **Citizenship**
Speaking and listening	Making plans and investigating. Sharing ideas and experiences. Commenting and reporting. Working in role. Speaking to different people. Varying speech to different circumstances. Taking account of listeners. Persuading. Explaining. Questioning.
PSHE and Citizenship	Personal hygiene. Keeping safe. Problem solving. Helping and caring for others. Working together.

Resources	Felt pens, large picture of shop front (see Figure 4.1). Optional props for baker: apron, wooden spoon. Letter from the Queen (see Figures 4.2 and 4.3). Optional props for the King: cloak, crown.
Time	Minimum of one hour. Could be broken into shorter sections at any point. Possibility of a whole or a half-day if the additional activities are included.

Notes

1. This drama is ideal for younger children and/or those inexperienced in drama because it engages the children as one group throughout. The teacher maintains close control of the unfolding dramatic fiction to which the children can contribute their own ideas.
2. The teacher takes two roles: the baker and the King.

Drama activities

1. Let's talk about bakeries (5 minutes)

[Discussion]
Introduce the session by leading a general discussion about bakers' shops.

We're going to tell a story today and it's going to be about a baker's shop.

Does anyone know where you buy bread?

Supermarkets do sell bread, you're quite right, but can you think of a special little shop?

This may be difficult for some young children, but you can introduce the idea of the baker's shop and the baker who makes the bread and cakes if necessary.

What else do you buy in the shop?

What is your favourite bread/cake/biscuit?

2. Drawing the shop window (10 minutes)

[Collective drawing]
Use a pre-prepared shop front outline. Place the outline and the felt pens in the centre of the circle of children. Children draw pictures of

their favourite cake, bread or biscuit into the outline of the window (see Figure 4.1).

Keep the dialogue going while the children are coming one or two at a time into the centre to draw their pictures:

What have you chosen as your favourite?

What colour is the icing?

Has the bun got cherries on the top?

What does it taste like?

What does it feel like to touch?

Figure 4.1 The baker's shop

3. The empty shop window (5 minutes)

[Storytelling]
Use the completed picture of the shop window as you begin to tell the story that should include the following points:

- The baker's shop is in a small village.
- Every morning the children stop to look in the window at the cakes on their way to school. Mr Baker often makes extra biscuits for them to put in their lunchboxes for snacks.

- Mr Baker has baked there for as long as anyone can remember. Everyone knows him. He is friendly and well liked.

One morning, the children looked in the window and it was...(turn over the paper to show the blank side)...empty!

4. What has happened to Mr Baker? (5 minutes)

[Class discussion]
Children discuss possible reasons for the empty window, for example, burglary, Mr Baker has died, he's still asleep. Accept all of these suggestions and say that any of them could have happened.

5. Children meet Mr Baker (10 minutes)

[Planning roles defining space; teacher in role]
Tell the children that they are going to be the children in the story and that they will be able to find out what has happened to Mr Baker. Set up the space together by deciding where the door of the shop will be and where they are going to stand to look through the window. Decide who will knock on the door and whether they will shout through the letterbox. Tell the children that in the next part of the story you are going to be Mr Baker and that you will wait in a certain place until you hear them call out a given phrase. You may decide to wear an apron or carry a wooden spoon to indicate when you are in role.

Teacher in role as Mr Baker hobbles to the door clutching his back and muttering:

Oh dear me. I wonder who this can be? Oh dear. Ouch. I'm coming...
(He painfully unbolts the door and smiles weakly at the children)...
Hello everyone. How nice to see you. Oh dear.

Hopefully, someone will ask what the matter is and why the shop isn't open today. Mr Baker explains that he has a bad back. He strained it lifting a bag of flour yesterday. The doctor has told him to rest for a few days. The problem is that he has no one to help him so he won't be able to cook anything or open the shop for a while. Usually the children offer to lend a hand but Mr Baker will need to be persuaded that they know something about cooking before he agrees to their kind offer. Ask them about any previous cooking they have done at home. Do they know what 'ingredients' are? Do they know what goes in the middle of doughnuts or on the top of birthday cakes?

6. Helping in the kitchen (10–15 minutes)

[Whole class improvisation]
Mr Baker leads the children through the shop and into his kitchen. He asks them if they know what to be careful of in the kitchen and reinforces some simple safety rules. He proudly shows them around his kitchen, pointing out the shelves lined with jars of scrumptious toppings, the cupboards full of equipment and the drawers containing the utensils.

Can you see what's in that jar up there?

Do mind those sacks of flour.

What do you think I keep in my fridge?

How many recipe books can you see on this shelf?

Open the drawer in front of you and tell me what utensils you can see inside.

Can everyone hold up a wooden spoon for me?

What do we need to do before we start cooking?

Why do we need to wash our hands?

Turn on the tap in front of you and let me see you scrub under your nails!

You'd better choose a coloured apron from this cupboard. What colour have you got? Help one another to tie the aprons. That's good.

What shall we cook today? Why don't you choose your favourite bread or cake to make? I'll help you if you need me.

The children work individually or in pairs to make their cakes and Mr Baker hobbles round giving help and advice:

You need some more flour in there; it's too sloppy!

How many eggs are you putting in?

What kind of jam are you putting in your tarts?

Put the tray on that table and I will put it in the oven for you.

Why don't you try making some biscuits now?

When you are finished go and sit in my sitting room and help yourself to a cup of juice and a biscuit.

When all the children are sitting down enjoying their drinks, Mr Baker sits with them and asks individuals questions about what they have made and how they got on.

7. A letter arrives from the palace with a request (5 minutes)

[Teacher in role]
Suddenly, Mr Baker hears a knock at the back door and hobbles over to open it. He finds that the postman has delivered a letter (see Figure 4.2). He holds the letter and peers at the envelope looking scared to open it.

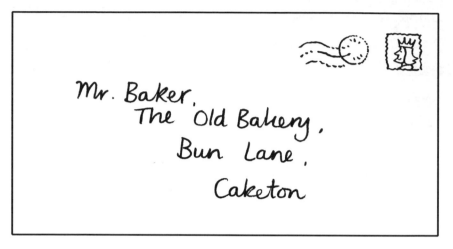

Figure 4.2 The letter from the palace

Who is it for?

I don't get many letters.

How do you know it's for me?

Can you help me to read what it says; I haven't got my glasses?

The letter is written on a piece of paper shaped like a crown and asks Mr Baker to bake a special cake for the King's birthday (see Figure 4.3).

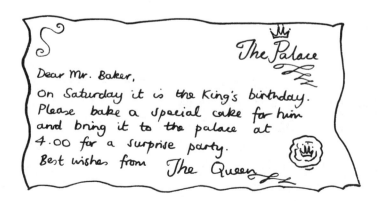

Figure 4.3 The request from the Queen

Mr Baker says that it is a great honour and it is a real shame that he won't be able to make the cake because of his bad back. He is very sad and sighs deeply.

Hopefully, his helpers will volunteer, but again he will need persuading that they know enough to bake such an important cake. Possible designs are discussed.

Additional activity
The cakes could be designed individually, in pairs or groups as an out of drama time activity. The designs could then be brought back into the drama and presented. The group can choose a favourite design or the teacher can narrate how the decision was made. For example:

After a great deal of discussion about the designs they decided to make a chocolate cake in the shape of a crown, with pink icing and 56 candles.

8. Making the King's birthday cake (5 minutes)

[Ritual]
Mr Baker asks his helpers to stand in a circle around his largest mixing bowl. He asks them to think of one special ingredient that they would like to put into the cake. This can be anything at all, from cherries to magic dust! We have had children wishing to add sausages and bacon to the mixture but every offering is treated with the same respect! Individually, children drop their ingredient into the bowl and say what it is for everyone to hear. Everyone stirs the mixture together a given number of times with everyone counting loudly.

9. Preparing for the party (5 minutes)

[Narration; teacher in role]
Teacher narrates:

The beautiful cake was baked and decorated by Mr Baker's friends. When Saturday came, Mr Baker was still too ill to go out so he asked the children if they could take the cake to the palace for him.

Teacher puts on apron and in role as Mr Baker says how pleased he is that the children are going to take the cake and that he is very proud of them. He asks them what they are going to wear to the party and he also asks whether they know the polite way of addressing the King and Queen when they meet them. Different expressions for greeting royalty and bows/curtseys can be practised if required!

10. The King's birthday party (10 minutes)

[Collective storytelling; teacher in role]
Teacher narrates with children adding detail:

The children arrived at the palace with the cake and were shown in to a huge ballroom where the party was to take place. They looked around the room and they could see ... and some golden ... (Ask individual children to supply appropriate words to describe the room) ... The children were feeling very ... as they waited. They had never met the King before but they had heard that he was ... After a while they heard footsteps approaching. They stood up and waited for the door to open.

Tell the children that you are going to be the King in the next part of the drama. Simple costume or props can be used to indicate this change of role.

Teacher in role as the King enters the room looking glum and holding his face. Rub your jaw and speak as though you had a mouth full of cotton wool. (Try not to make the King too similar to Mr Baker. They are both in pain but should walk and behave distinctly.)

Greet the children in a very half-hearted fashion, not rudely but distractedly.

Hopefully the children will greet the King as previously practised, if not the King must start the conversation by groaning and asking who they are and why they are there.

The King speaks miserably saying how kind they are but how he couldn't possibly eat any cake. He has terrible toothache. He has never heard of a 'tendist' and has never used a toothbrush. (The King is unfamiliar with the word dentist and the children have to correct his mispronunciation.) He wondered why the Queen had given him a small brush and some mint-flavoured paste for his birthday. The children tell the King how to look after his teeth; advising and demonstrating correct brushing techniques. He is so pleased with the result of his clean teeth, as the brushing has dislodged something stuck in his gum. He decides that the party can go ahead after all. The children can suggest games and sing appropriate songs (usually 'Happy Birthday!').

11. The party is over (5 minutes)

[Narration]
Teacher narrates the end of the story:

The party was a great success and the children had a wonderful time playing ... and ... with the King. The next day they went to tell Mr Baker all about the party and how they had helped the King to look after his teeth.

12. Reflection (5 minutes)

[Discussion]
Ask the children to sit down and discuss the story. Who did the children help in the story? Was the King as they had expected him to be? What did they tell Mr Baker when they saw him?

1. Writing activities
    These activities can be undertaken individually, in pairs, groups or as whole class shared writing:
    (a) Writing a thank you letter to the King.
    (b) Writing out the recipe for the birthday cake.
    (c) Noting down a set of instructions for the King to remind him how to brush his teeth.
    (d) Designing a poster advertising Mr Baker's shop.
    (e) Making a character study for the King and the baker.
    (f) Designing birthday cards for the King.
    (g) Composing an invitation inviting the King to visit the bakery.
2. Drama activities
    (a) Set up an imaginative play corner as the bakery or the palace.
    (b) Make puppets and use them to retell the story.
3. Art and technology activities
    (a) Draw or paint pictures of the characters or the cake.
    (b) Bake a birthday cake.

Additional possibilities

Chapter 5

Life Cycles
Science

Helena has never lived in the country before. Her flat in the city was great for views, but no good for learning about gardens and nature. When Helena moves into a tiny home in the country she is upset by the changes that occur in her garden. She doesn't know where the butterflies have gone, nor why there are only flowers on the apple trees and no apples. The children are invited to help Helena understand the life cycles at play, and teach her how to take care of her garden.

Age group	5–8 years
Curriculum area focus	**Science** Life cycles. Plants and growth. Living things.
Speaking and listening	Taking into account the needs of listeners. Explanatory language. Ordering and clarifying. Extending ideas in the light of discussion. Gaining and maintaining the interest of different audiences. Asking relevant questions.
PSHE and Citizenship	Sharing opinions and explaining views. Problem solving. Environmental concerns. Caring about other people's feelings.

Resources	None.
Time	This drama can be completed in one to one and a half hours.

Notes

1. This lesson was prepared to follow initial work on life cycles to help a teacher assess how much the children had understood, to engage children in applying what they had covered to other contexts, and to reaffirm learning.
2. Through this dramatic encounter, children share their knowledge, combine it with that of the others, and make sense of it through grappling to answer Helena's questions.
3. The teacher playing Helena should appear perplexed and lacking in basic knowledge. At the same time Helena is determined to understand, and therefore asks searching questions. For example: 'But how can it be a chrysalis at one moment and then a butterfly the next?' We have found that with younger children, she can appear to understand almost nothing and therefore she requires the children to explain the very basics first. It may be that the children need to do some research or drawings to clarify the processes they are trying to explain.

1. Introducing Helena (5 minutes)

Drama activities

[Teacher narration]

> Helena had lived in a busy city all her life. Her flat was at the very top of a high-rise block of flats. She was ready to retire and dreamed of having a really beautiful garden. Although she had enjoyed the views from the flat, she was sad never to have had a garden and wanted something really special. She only wanted a very small house, but, oh, how she dreamed of a lovely garden. It took a while taking train trips in different directions, but at last she found it: a tiny house with a perfect garden.

2. Creating the garden (20 minutes)

[Discussion; movement and sound collage]
Ask the children what the perfect garden might be like. What might be in it – a pond, lilies, roses, rabbits? Teacher continues questioning:

> What sort of flowers?

> Are they scented?

> Whereabouts in the garden do they grow?

Through this discussion the children generate an idea of the garden. From here, they create it, agreeing first where significant features are.

Is the pond in the middle?

What did we say was growing near the pond?

Where will the rose bush be?

In pairs or small groups, the children need to:

- Decide what they will represent in the garden, such as the apple tree, the pond, the buttercups.
- Discuss words to describe what they are representing. A three-word minimum is a helpful limitation. Examples are: old, gnarled apple tree; scrambling, reaching, climbing roses.
- Become the feature. It could be still if they are representing a rockery or it could involve minimal movement. We have seen two children create a lily that opened by the children leaning and waving their arms back.
- Consider whereabouts they should be in the space, given the landmarks agreed earlier.
- Practise saying the words while in their positions.

Once the garden is created, explain that you will take the role of Helena walking around her garden. When she walks by, or stands by a pair/group, they should whisper their words. As she moves nearer the words get a bit louder, and as she moves away they get quieter and then fade away.

Teacher mimes opening a back door and walking outside, delighted, into the garden. She moves between the groups, perhaps dropping her hand into the pond and smelling the flowers. The words are whispered as she moves around the space, back and forth revisiting the different garden features. This creates a wonderful collage of sound as well as the physical picture. Finally, after a long happy look, Helena returns to her house.

3. Helena is sad (5 minutes)

[Narration]

That summer was very happy for Helena. She spent much of her time in the garden. Autumn arrived, then winter and into spring, but during this time, things had changed. The neighbours hardly saw Helena. She spent no time in her garden at all. They couldn't understand it. Helena just stayed in her house. They began to peer through the window to see if she was all right. She was just sitting in her tiny room. She looked so sad. Some even thought they saw her crying. It was so strange, such a change from the Helena of before. Though the neighbours were worried, none of them had yet gone in.

4. Helping Helena (10–30 minutes)

[Teacher in role and whole class improvisation]
Tell the children that the neighbours decide to go to see Helena to try to find out what is wrong. The children will take the roles of the neighbours. Some discussion about what to say and how to approach Helena would be helpful.

What should we say first?

What sort of mood do you think we should present?

How will she know that we mean well?

What sort of voices should we use since she is upset?

Explain that once you are sitting on a chair, you will be Helena and the drama can begin with one of the children knocking at an imaginary door. One child can be chosen to do this.

Helena is reluctant to speak to them. She is sure they don't want to come in. She is not in the mood for visitors. Once they are in, she only gradually responds to questions and explains that she is disappointed. She loved the garden, but it's all changed. She doesn't know much about gardens, but even she can see that it is not how it was. She presents particular anxieties. The children will deal with each one as it comes up. She may ask them many questions to help understand their explanations. Each time they will think that Helena should be happy and then she introduces another anxiety that they need to help her understand. The reasons for Helena's sadness are outlined below. The order in which they are discussed is not important.

Problem 1: apple blossom ➜ fruit

Last September there were lots of apples on the trees. It was wonderful. She used to pick one every day. But now there aren't any at all! The apple trees have got flowers on which are quite pretty, but where are the apples? She thought that the tree had died around Christmas because it went completely bare.

Problem 2: frogspawn ➜ tadpoles ➜ frogs

She used to love watching the frogs around the pond, but now they are nowhere to be seen. In fact, the pond looks pretty revolting because it is full of slimy, jelly-mould stuff covered in nasty black spots. Helena can't believe the children's explanation that this will become frogs. It hasn't even got legs! And concerning tadpoles, she thinks they need their heads examined because frogs don't have tails!

Problem 3: caterpillars → chrysalis → butterflies

Helena misses the butterflies. They used to look so pretty. Why have they left the garden? What has she done wrong? She used to sit beside the hedge and watch them fly around the sunflowers. Now she wouldn't even sit by the hedge because it is covered with squidgy green hairy things that walk in a strange loopy way.

Problem 4: eggs → baby birds

You may have had enough after three problems, but this one always gives the children a smile. Helena is embarrassed that the children must think her a bit foolish for not understanding these things. However, she does know about eggs. As soon as she saw them in the nest she knew exactly what to do with them, but they have been in the fridge for two weeks and they still haven't hatched!

5. Clearing the garden (15 minutes)

[Improvisation]

Helena thanks them for their advice and asks them if there are things she should be doing to care for her garden.

Should I move the leaves or will they keep the grass and flower beds warm?

Does it matter that there are odd things growing between my rose beds?

What can I do about the privet hedge being so tall and jagged on top that it looks ugly?

The children offer or are asked to help with the garden. They all choose which jobs they will do, such as weeding, hedge cutting, raking the leaves and so on. Finally, Helena thanks them for their help.

6. All's well that ends well (10 minutes)

[Recreating the garden]

To round off this drama, the children can recreate the garden as they did in activity 2, using themselves to represent different features.

When they are still and in position, Helena walks around the garden saying how pleased she is that she has learned so much about her garden and about how things grow. She could give some detail of what she has learnt if the children need some points reinforced or clarified. If they were shaky on how a chrysalis is made, for example, she can explain it to herself aloud, perhaps as though she is looking at one. In this way, more information can be given.

1. Art: shared class drawing
   The teacher and class can complete a large drawing of the garden (as constructed in activity 6) discussing approximate distances between the features.
2. Science: research and chart making task
   Children can make charts to show the life cycle of frogs, fruit or butterflies. Pairs could cover different life forms. Research for illustrations may be necessary.
3. Maths: individual planning, counting and measuring
   Design a garden on squared paper. An allocation of a particular number of squares can be given for the garden and a list of features that can be included in the plan. Each feature could be worth a given number of squares, for example, pond = 5 squares, rose bed = 3 squares.

Additional possibilities

Chapter 6

Red Riding Hood
Crime and punishment

This drama begins with the familiar story. Mother sends Red Riding Hood (RRH) on an important errand. Grandmother, who lives on the other side of the wood, is poorly and RRH takes a basket of goodies to cheer her up. However, when Red Riding Hood arrives at her grandmother's house she realises that a wolf occupies her grandmother's bed. A passing woodcutter rescues Red Riding Hood and her grandmother, and the wolf receives a well-deserved punishment.

This incident causes a great deal of distress and anxiety to the local villagers and forest dwellers. Does the wolf deserve to be punished? Is he sorry for what he has done? How will his family cope without him? Will safety arrangements be changed in the forest after this incident?

Age group	5–11 years. The main section of the drama can be used with KS1 children very successfully. This does not imply that the work is too easy for KS2 pupils but the children will respond differently to the tasks depending on maturity. There are suggestions for further KS2 activities included at the end of the main drama. These activities demand more specific drama or linguistic skills.
Curriculum area focus	**English** Traditional tales, Storytelling.
Speaking and listening	Telling stories real and imagined. Describing events and experiences. Making plans and investigating.

Sharing ideas and experiences.
Commenting and reporting.
Working in role.
Speaking to different people.
Varying speech to different circumstances.
Taking account of listeners.
Persuading, explaining, questioning.

PSHE and citizenship

Recognising what is right and wrong, what is fair and unfair.
Sharing opinions and explaining views.
Keeping safe.
Recognising how their behaviour affects other people.
Problem solving.
Helping and caring for others.
Working together.
Considering moral and social dilemmas.
Realising the consequences of aggressive behaviour.

Resources

A basket for Granny's goodies to be put into/or a large piece of paper with Granny's basket drawn on it (see Figure 6.1).
Felt pens.
Small pieces of paper and glue or 'Post-its' may be required for activity 2.
Optional props for Granny and wolf (a shawl and a hat, for example).

Time

Most activities take between five and ten minutes for each separate activity. The drama as it is written can easily be split up in to the separate activities and be used during the first shared section of the Literacy Hour. There is also the possibility of longer sessions, for example, a half-day drama session, whole day, or over a longer number of drama sessions spread over a few weeks if all of the additional activities are included.

Notes

1. This drama uses the well-known traditional tale and explores certain issues from it. As class teacher you have to decide whether you want Granny and Red Riding Hood to be eaten by the wolf; or is Granny hiding in the wardrobe and is RRH rescued just in time? We usually have them both eaten alive and whole, not chewed by the wolf, so that the woodcutter can turn the wolf upside-down and shake him – they fall out unharmed. Also, in our 'sanitised' version, the woodcutter does not kill the wolf, so we are able to meet him later on and talk to him. An added twist is that the wolf is a family man and we can meet members of his family in the drama.

2. The teacher maintains close control of the unfolding dramatic fiction in which the children are encouraged to contribute their own ideas to a well-known story.

3. The drama is structured using a series of drama conventions that can stand alone as one off activities. This can be a 'pick and mix' drama session or can be followed straight through if time allows.

Drama activities

1. Telling our version of the story (10 minutes)

[Collective storytelling]

If you can find an appropriate written text then that can be used, but an oral retelling is preferable as the children can help to tell the story. This will give them more collective ownership of the tale. What follows is based on the authors' version of the story.

Introduce the work by leading a storytelling session to make sure everyone is using the same version of the story as the basis of the drama. As there are clearly hundreds of alternative versions of the traditional story, emphasise that this is our special version and it may not be the same as other versions that the children have heard. Start with the traditional opening and set the scene.

Once upon a time, there lived a little girl whose name was Elizabeth. Everyone who knew Elizabeth called her Little Red Riding Hood because she always wore a red cloak with a hood that her granny had made for her. She lived with her mother and father in a little cottage in the middle of a wood.

After modelling the storytelling technique for a short while, give children opportunities to supply words or phrases to finish your sentences. Tell the children that you will look directly at the person who you want to give the next part of the story. This form of collective storytelling involves all of the children and ensures that they listen to the story because no one knows who will be asked to give the next idea.

At the specific moment in the story when Red Riding Hood is packing the basket of goodies, use the basket or the prepared picture of Granny's basket for the next activity.

2. What goodies shall we take to Granny? (10 minutes)

[Collective drawing; ritual]
Children discuss what might be put in the basket. If you have a basket, each child draws a picture of an object to put in it. If you are using a picture of a basket, childen can either draw objects onto the prepared picture, or they can draw objects onto 'Post-its' to be stuck onto the prepared picture (see Figure 6.1).

Figure 6.1 A basket to fill with goodies for Granny

Children stand around the basket in a circle and come forward one at a time to place items in the basket, while announcing what it is they are putting in:

I am putting a magazine in the basket for Granny.

A hot water bottle.

Medicine.

I am giving Granny some flowers.

I think Granny would like a video to cheer her up.

The pictures are then stuck onto the collective picture of the basket.

3. Finish the story (5 minutes)

[Storytelling]
Continue the collective storytelling including the following points:

- RRH is warned by her mother not to talk to strangers.
- She stops to talk to some of her friends in the forest and the wolf overhears their conversation.

- The door to Granny's cottage is ajar when she arrives and the cottage is in darkness.
- The wolf swallows RRH in one piece without chewing her at all.
- The woodcutter shakes the wolf and RRH falls out unharmed, followed closely by Granny.
- Wolf is taken to prison or to the zoo depending on how you feel about his behaviour.

4. Shall I tell you what happened to me yesterday? (10 minutes)

[Storytelling in role; discussion]
Tell the children that you are going to tell the story again as if you were one of the characters. Use some simple props or costume to indicate that you are in role as Granny. Sit on a chair which is perhaps draped with material and can be known as the 'storyteller's chair' to make it sound a little more exciting. In role as Granny, recall the events that happened in your cottage yesterday. It is quite fun if Granny is not a 'stereotypical' grandmother and is actually rather cheeky. She was not frightened by her ordeal and is thankful that the wolf didn't chew her up. What she didn't like was the smell of curry/garlic/salt and vinegar crisps in his stomach and also that his teeth were not brushed and were rotting.

Talk about the different viewpoint. How would it be different if the wolf had told the story?

Additional activity
In groups of four, children tell the story round the group in role as one of the other main characters – wolf, RRH, the woodcutter. How are these stories different?

5. Who will you be in the story? (10 minutes)

[Developing roles for the children]
Tell the children that they are all going to be characters in the story and they can choose who they would like to be.

Unfortunately, the children cannot choose to be one of the main characters – RRH, wolf, woodcutter, Granny – but they can decide to be someone who knows Granny or one of the other characters. They might be one of the people who live in the wood, perhaps a friend of Granny's or even the local postman. More experienced practitioners may consider giving children the opportunity of taking on the roles of woodland animal friends of RRH (such as rabbits, owl, fox). However, this may be difficult for less experienced groups to cope with sensibly. Clearly the children would be asked to behave in a humanised manner, not growling and crawling on the floor! It is great fun to include these characters though, as they add another dimension to the story. Particularly useful characters are Mrs Wolf and the wolf children.

Ask the children to tell the person next to them who they are going to be in the drama and then to tell the whole group. They need to make it clear how they know the other characters from the wood and you may have to help them through some direct questioning. Older children can introduce themselves to the group in role.

I am Mrs Wolf. I'm married to the wolf that ate Granny. He's not a bad chap really. I don't know why he did it.

I'm Doris Starling. I know Granny from Bingo. She's a lovely lady.

I live in the village and run the shop. I know everyone who lives here.

6. Talking to Red Riding Hood (10 minutes)

[Hot seating the teacher in role]
Tell the children that it is a couple of days after the incident and Red Riding Hood is feeling very twitchy about what happened. She is afraid that some other awful things may happen. Ask the children if they will talk to her about what happened and try to reassure her. First they may ask some questions about the incident, and then go on to reassure her about things to boost her confidence. What would they like to ask? Frame some questions in pairs or as a whole group. Perhaps write them down on the board to refer to. What can they say to reassure RRH? How should they approach her? What tone of voice should they use?

Children in role as neighbours talk to teacher in role as Red Riding Hood and find out more information about her adventure with the wolf. They then go on to coax her into a walk in the woods or a visit to see some friends or something else to give her confidence.

In a KS2 class, a child could take on this role successfully.

7. Collecting the information (5 minutes)

[Role on the wall]
Gather together the information that has been collected about the event in the form of a simple role on the wall. This involves drawing a figure to represent RRH on a large sheet of paper and writing in the information that has been discussed (see Figure 6.2).

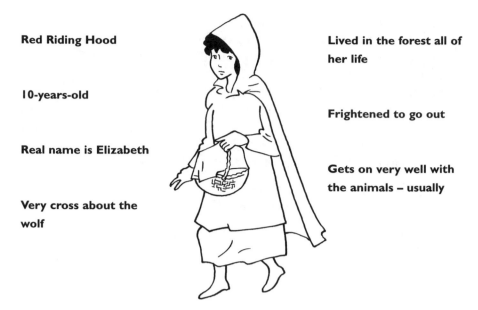

Figure 6.2   Role on the wall for RRH

8. You have been a very bad wolf (5 minutes)

[Thought tunnel]
Tell the children that they are going to be able to tell the wolf what they think of his behaviour. Give some examples in order to avoid inappropriate statements!

> *I think you should be ashamed of yourself.*
>
> *Why did you do it?*
>
> *I wonder how long you'll be in prison?*
>
> *What did they taste like?*

Children form two parallel lines facing into the path between the lines. Teacher in role as wolf walks down the path and each character has the opportunity to express his or her thoughts about him. The wolf cannot reply to the comments and questions and walks slowly along the path looking miserable (see Figure 6.3).

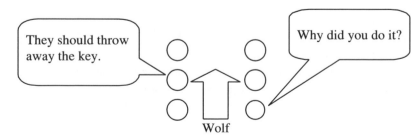

Figure 6.3   The thought tunnel

9. I'm in trouble now! (5 minutes)

[Thought tunnel]
In this activity the children are asked to speak the thoughts of the wolf as he walks down the corridor towards the police cell, the cage in the zoo or wherever you decide to put him after his crime! Discuss possibilities about what might be going around in his mind first so everyone feels that they have something to say. Teacher in role walks slowly along the corridor and his thoughts are spoken.

I wish I hadn't done it.

I'm in big trouble.

Still, I was really hungry.

I wasn't going to do it but I couldn't resist.

It was typical of that nosy woodcutter to barge in at the wrong moment.

I'm sorry.

How will my wife and seven cubs get on without me?

I hope the judge is lenient.

Alternative activity
A similar activity to this could be done with the children sitting in a square around the wolf to represent the walls of the prison cell, the bars of the cage or wherever you decide he is sitting. The teacher in role as wolf could pace around while the children speak his thoughts as before (see Figure 6.4).

Figure 6.4   An alternative to a thought tunnel

10. Finding out more information (10 minutes)

[Interviewing]
In pairs, the children are given the task of interviewing and being interviewed. The pairs could be:

- Local newspaper reporter interviewing Red Riding Hood's mother.
- Police constable interviewing the woodcutter.
- An animal behaviourist interviewing the wolf.

All of these combinations demand different types of language to be used by the children and explore different viewpoints.

11. What should be done about the wolf's behaviour? (10–15 minutes)

[Meeting and teacher in role]
Tell the children that there is going to be a meeting arranged to discuss local problems. Children in role as villagers or woodland dwellers are invited to a meeting in the village hall or the clearing in the wood to discuss the incident at Granny's cottage and other important local issues. Ask the children to set up the space as if there was to be a formal meeting. Chairs can be used to form rows, otherwise sit on the floor.

Teacher takes on the role of an authority figure such as a mayor, vicar, neighbourhood watch coordinator or head teacher and welcomes everyone to the meeting. (In a KS2 class, a child could take on this role successfully and perhaps be supported by one or two other children in minor lead roles.)

There was a terrible incident in the wood last week and I know that many of you have said that you are worried that this might only be the start. Has anybody got anything that they want to say about the incident with the wolf or any other incidents that they know about?

Chair of the meeting invites comments and questions from the meeting.

At the end of this meeting tell the group that there is a visitor who would like to come and speak to them.

Teacher now takes the role of the wolf's wife. She has been to visit him. She is able to tell the meeting that the wolf is really sorry and that he was over-excited/just playing/was really hungry, or whatever, and wants to be forgiven. He knows that he has done wrong but wishes that he could be given a second chance.

The children have to decide whether they will be able to forgive the wolf and if so what are their conditions. There is no right or wrong decision and it may be that there is no definitive decision made by the meeting. The wolf's wife can leave at any point to let the meeting consider what to do.

12. Reflecting on the story (5 minutes)

[Statementing]
Each member of the group has the opportunity to say what he thinks

about the wolf by making a statement about him. A chair is put into the middle of a circle (on which we imagine that the wolf is sitting). One at a time the children come forward towards the chair and speak their thoughts about the story.

You were very naughty.

I think you feel sorry now.

Don't do it again.

I don't think you are really sorry.

Will the woods ever be safe again?

1. Telling the story in pictures (20–30 minutes)

Additional drama activities

[Storyboard or list; still images; thought tap; storytelling using still images]
Tell the children that they are going to tell the story in pictures, like the pictures in a storybook. They are going to make the pictures in the form of still images, so you may need to remind them that pictures do not move or speak!

Ask the children to think about the key moments in the story. Make a list of these in chronological order or fill in a simple storyboard.

In groups of three or four, children are given a specific moment in the story to show as an image. All of the children in the group will need to be involved in the image so some may need to represent furniture or trees, or one may be designated to speak the caption (see below). The pictures could show:

- Packing the basket of goodies for Granny.
- Leaving home and setting off through the forest.
- Meeting the wolf in the clearing in the wood.
- Arriving at Granny's cottage.
- Inside the wolf's tummy.
- The arrival of the woodcutter.
- The Police/RSPCA take the wolf away.
- The wolf in prison/the zoo being visited by his family.
- Granny being visited by her friends.
- The woodcutter being given a bravery award by the mayor.

Ask each group to decide on a caption for their picture. What caption would go underneath this picture in a book?

The groups then show their pictures in a random order and everyone else reads the picture to discover which moment is being shown. The captions are spoken out loud or could have been written on paper and revealed at an appropriate moment.

You can find out more about what is happening in the picture by thought tapping or speaking to any of the people in it. At Key Stage 1 the questioning can be fairly simple such as:

What can you see in front of you?

How are you feeling at this moment?

What do you think will happen now?

What are you saying at this moment?

What do you think about the fact that a wolf has eaten you?

At Key Stage 2 the questioning needs to be more challenging and complex for example:

Do you think it is wise to send a young girl out into the woods alone?

What do you think your punishment will be for this crime?

Describe your reaction to this event.

Now ask the children to decide in which order the pictures would go in a book. Tell the children that you are going to use the pictures to retell the story and that at the right moment in the story each group will make the appropriate picture and read or speak the caption that goes with it.

The still image pictures are then put into the right order chronologically and shown again with the teacher miming the turning over of pages in a large book to reveal each new picture and narrating a shortened version of the story to incorporate all of the pictures. For example, mime holding a large book and reading the title:

The story of Little Red Riding Hood … (Mime reading the first page).

Once upon a time there was a little girl who had to visit her sick grandmother who lived on the other side of the wood. The girl helped her mother to pack a basket of goodies to take with her.

Group 1 make their still image of the basket being packed and one person speaks their caption:

Granny will love all of these things.

After the image has been shown the group sits down to watch the others.

Note that this activity has a real feeling of ritual. There is definite tension created here as the children strive to get their image right and a real sense of whole class cooperation is built up. It can be practised and refined and possibly performed as a piece for an assembly or school play.

2. Sculpting the wolf (10 minutes)

The teacher or a child is sculpted by the children to represent the wolf at given moments in the story. Choose three different points in the story such as the beginning, the moment of capture and in his cage or prison cell. These can be focused on to investigate the use of body posture and gesture to convey the feelings of characters. Depending on how brave or trusting you are, either follow instructions given by individuals to refine your position or children can come forward and physically manipulate parts of your body until an agreed sculpture of the wolf is seen.

At the beginning of the story, when he meets RRH in the wood, how is he going to be feeling?

How will he look to show that he is feeling happy and excited?

Shall we see him standing or sitting?

How will he stand then?

What about his paws?

Will his head be hanging down like this or up like this?

What about the expression on his face?

Is his back straight enough for this moment in the story?

Additional possibilities

1. Writing activities
These activities can be undertaken individually, in pairs, groups or as whole class shared writing:
    (a) Writing the end of the story.
    (b) Writing part of the story from the viewpoint of a chosen character.
    (c) Doing a character study of the wolf or RRH.
    (d) Listing rules for wolf behaviour.
    (e) Writing out directions to Granny's cottage.
    (f) Writing a letter to the wolf in prison.
    (g) Designing a get well card for Granny.
    (h) Composing a newspaper report.
    (i) Doing labels for the goodies in the basket.
2. Other activities
    (a) Drawing individual pictures of the basket of goodies.
    (b) Setting up an imaginative play area as Granny's cottage or the wood.
    (c) Making a collection of different book versions of the story.
    (d) Collecting other wolf stories.

Chapter 7

Building the Pyramid
History

An ancient Egyptian architect has a very important meeting planned with the Pharaoh. Unfortunately, he is sick and unable to go. He needs the help of the children to find out details of the new building the Pharaoh wants him to construct. They need to consider what the architect would need to know, such as the size, the materials and the purpose of the building. Once this information has been reported back to the architect, the children create images depicting farming scenes using pictures from pyramid walls. Finally, they meet the farmers who are recruited to build the pyramid and discover the conditions under which they worked.

Age group	6–9 years
Curriculum area focus	**History** World study of a past society: Ancient Egypt. Design: buildings and their purposes.
Speaking and listening	Speaking with confidence in a range of contexts. Adapting speech for a range of audience. Reporting back events. Asking relevant questions. Recalling important features of what's been heard. Group planning.
PSHE and Citizenship	Helping others. Listening to people and working cooperatively.
Resources	Pyramid pictures (see Figures 7.1, 7.2, 7.3). Embalming instructions (see activity 7).

	Large sheets of sugar paper and marker pens.
Time	This work will take a minimum of two hours but could take up to three.

1. This drama focuses on the construction of pyramids, their design and purposes. However, along the way, other information about Ancient Egypt emerges, such as farming practices and conditions for the rich and poor. Some teachers have used this history project as the basis for a design activity.
2. This drama involves whole group drama and small group activities.
3. The teacher takes various roles to challenge the children's learning at different stages.
4. Historical information required for the drama is provided.
5. The story was constructed after reading David Macauley's *Pyramid* (1976) published by Collins, London.
6. You may choose to do only the first meeting of the children and the Pharaoh. This provides the children with an enormous amount of information and can be followed by work on design plans or further historical study.

1. Providing historical context (10 minutes)

[Game]
Explain that the drama is about a time far in the past: the times of Ancient Egypt, which are over 1000 years BC and stretch until 3000 years before we begin numbering our years in the West. This game helps to imagine a time long ago.

Standing in a large circle children think of an object. A child crosses the circle announcing the object, for example, a kettle. The children must then call 'yes' or 'no' depending on whether they think the object would have been around in Ancient Egypt. So, kettle would obviously get a call of 'no', while pots, tools and clothes would all get a 'yes'. When the child has crossed the circle and the call has been made, he takes the place of another child who then moves across towards someone else, saying another object.

2. Looking at Mahnud and the Pharaoh (10 minutes)

[Discussion]
Look at the picture in Figure 7.1 and talk with the children about it.

Who do you think is more important?

What has the sitting figure got on his head?

55

Why might they be wearing so little?

What is a pharaoh?

Finally, tell them that in their story the standing figure is Mahnud Hotep, who is a very good and hardworking architect, and the seated figure is his Pharaoh, who has told Mahnud that he wants a new building built in his kingdom of Egypt.

3. The children are asked to help Mahnud (15 minutes)

[In role discussion]
In this activity the teacher and children take on no distinct roles but they are clearly not themselves, because they speak as though they are in Ancient Egypt.

Explain to the children that Mahnud has some very bad luck. He is sick and he is meant to have a meeting with the Pharaoh today to talk about the new building. He is too ill to go, but is terrified that he may lose the work if he fails to take the details from the Pharaoh. He needs the job to support his family and this job would secure him work for some time.

He wonders if the children would be prepared to go to the Pharaoh in his place and to find out all they can about what sort of building the Pharaoh wants built. Mahnud would be very grateful to them. He really needs their help. (If they are reluctant, you could offer a share of the finances! We don't usually find it necessary.)

Once they have agreed to go, explain that you don't know what sort of things they need to ask about the building. Mahnud will obviously need very detailed information. Can they think of what they will need to find out? Some examples children give and possible teacher responses are shown below:

What is it to be made of? — Yes. I don't know. Maybe he wants a wooden building.

What does he want to use it for? — Good point. It could be for parties!

Where does he want it? — I hadn't thought of that! Mahnud will need to know.

When does it need to be built? — Of course! Mahnud may not have much time.

How much will he pay? — He will certainly want to know that!

How big does he want it? — Good question. He may want a little cosy place.

What will it look like? — Yeah! We need to ask that! Could be orange towers.

Tell them to find out all they can, and remind them to be polite to the Pharaoh! You can hear him coming!

Figure 7.1 The meeting

4. Meeting with the Pharaoh (15–45 minutes)

[Whole group improvisation]

Teacher in role as the Pharaoh enters with great dignity. You may hold your hands up, palms out, looking at the children before you are seated. Though not authentic, this adds a bit of ritual to the drama. Sit with your feet square in front of you, straight back, and hands flat on each knee.

The children will then ask their teacher for all the information that you want them to have! They will want to know all that you want to teach them. They want to know for Mahnud, rather than because it is on the curriculum, but the effect is the same: children learn all you can tell them about pyramids!

Make the children work for the information, not giving all the details at once. We have enjoyed playing quite a haughty pharaoh who wants his building slightly higher than his father's! We have also played pharaohs who really don't like to be bothered with these tedious details, but, well, will give them some of his precious time.

Ideas for answers to the most obvious questions are provided here:

What is it to be made of?

— Stone. Homes for our short lives on earth may be of mud, but for the eternal life after, the building must last. Stone it must be. It can be shipped from the quarry down the Nile. About 50,000 men will be needed to transport the stone from the quarry to the site.

(Boats and sledges were used to move the stone when there were no wheels.)

What do you want to use it for?

— For my body to rest. There my 'ba' soul will rest beside my mummified body and my 'ka' spirit will travel between my body on earth and the other world. There must be a secret passageway for my 'ka' spirit to leave and enter. It must be secret. No one must find their way in.

Where do you want it?

— On the west bank of the Nile, for there the sun sets, beginning its nightly journey into the other world. I will be nearer Ra, the sun god if the building is there.

When does it need to be built?

— I do not know when I will require this building. I know you have no time to waste since just to prepare the site and establish the foundations will take about seven years.

How much will you pay?

— Mahnud will be well paid. The farmers who will be carrying out the hard labour will be paid in food and clothes. They will be pleased for this since they cannot farm between July and November when the Nile floods.

How big do you want it?

— *Good question. 160 metres, please.*

What will it look like?

— *I wish it to be a perfect pyramid so that it represents four rays of the sun protecting me. This will link me to Ra, the god of the sun.*

This activity may take a short time, but if you have enough information to impart, it may be for as long as 45 minutes.

Macauley's book provides interesting detail, such as the stones having to be all the same size exactly, and each group of twenty working on the cutting of one stone would have their own mark on the stone. In this way, punishment could be given for any stone not perfectly cut.

5. Reporting back to Mahnud (30 minutes)

Children now need to assimilate and use the newly acquired information. Here are three possibilities. If you want to assess individual children's level of knowledge, activity (c) may be most appropriate.

(a) With a whole group improvisation
You may want to check out how much information the children have picked up. Asking them to tell Mahnud is an exciting way to do so. As Mahnud, you can ask about particular things that you need to know to jog their memories. You must not imply that you were there! You need to know the information rather than needing to tell it.

(b) By small group planning
Another possibility is to ask small groups to prepare plans and notes of information on large sheets of paper.

(c) With an individual writing task
Alternatively, children could individually write a report for Mahnud, giving him the details he requires.

6. Looking at pyramid pictures (15 minutes)

[Small group still images]
Explain to the children that they can now find out something about the work force, and that we know about the way the people farmed because of the paintings inside the pyramids. In small groups children are given copies of pyramid drawings depicting farm labourers at work (see Figures 7.2, 7.3). The groups must first work out what the labourers are actually doing and then create the picture themselves by taking the positions of the figures in the pictures.

Figure 7.2   Pyramid drawings

N. de Garis Davies 'Ancient Egyptian Paintings'. Reproduced by permission of the Syndics of CambridgeUniversity library

Figure 7.3   Pyramid drawings

N. de Garis Davies 'Ancient Egyptian Paintings'. Reproduced by permission of the Syndics of Cambridge University library

Once they have finished, arrange them in rows on four sides so that they seem to be the pictures on the walls of the pyramid.

Extension activity (20 minutes)
[Still images, presentation and teacher in role]
You may like to invite another class into the space as visitors to the ancient pyramid. You can take the role as guide to draw attention to the different activities depicted in the pictures. The visitors may like to invite the magic of the place by going up to figures and asking them about what they are doing. It is best to keep these one at a time.

7. Embalming the Pharaoh (30 minutes)

This activity can be done with the whole class, with the teacher as the embalming priest if the children are younger or less mature, or in groups as described below.

Invite the children to imagine that time has passed, the pyramid is just completed and the Pharaoh has died. Children are divided into groups, given the embalming details (see below) and asked to enact the process. One child in each group pretends to be the priest who was in charge of the embalming process. As they work, the priest is teaching new embalmers how to do the job properly. They can use their bags, coats or one of themselves as the Pharaoh being embalmed. The group must ensure that all the processes are included, and that all the information provided on embalming is given to the new embalmers. They can make their scene as serious or comical as they like. The new embalmers can be good learners or bad!

Thus, the making of a mummy took 70 days so the priest in the scene may say to his learners something like, 'Well, we will start today and, as I am sure you have been told, we will be doing this job for 70 days'.

Each of the three stages could be given to a different group and then performed in order.

Stage One

- The priest often wears a jackal mask during the embalming process. The jackal headed god is the god of mummification.
- Make a cut in the left side of the body to remove the organs that are likely to go bad, such as the stomach and lungs.
- A hook like a crochet hook is poked up the nostrils to remove the brain.
- The organs are to be placed into canopic jars. These are made of stone with lids depicting different gods, each protecting a different organ.

Stage Two

- Natron, a preserving salt collected from the desert lakes, is put inside the body.
- Stitch up the body.
- Clean the body.
- Rub sweet smelling liquid into the skin of the body to help preserve it.

Stage Three

- Wrap the body in linen bandages. The quality and amount of linen used depends on the wealth and status of the dead person. A pharaoh will obviously have the most.
- Amulets must be wrapped between the layers of linen. A special one must be placed over the heart, such as an amulet depicting the scarab beetle often found in tomb paintings.
- The mummy is placed in its case. The dead person's portrait is painted on the case so that when his 'ka' spirit returns it will recognise its own body.

Additional possibilities

1. Research and drawing
   Look up the stages of the mummification process. Draw diagrams to explain the process. Find out the meanings of some of the objects painted onto the case.
2. Research and group presentation
   Small groups find out about one particular pyramid and prepare a presentation of information to the others. In this way children will hear about several constructions, such as the step pyramid made for King Djoser in about 2650BC, and the Great Pyramid of King Khufu, which is big enough to enclose the main cathedrals of Milan, Rome, Florence and London!

Chapter 8

Land Tax

Geography and maths

The inhabitants of a small island grow all their own food. They rely on the land for everything they need. The land that they farm and use on the island is owned by a person known to the islanders as 'The Owner' to whom they must pay rent each year. The rent is paid with a certain percentage of produce from the land. The Owner's messenger is sent on a given day every year to collect the rent. All goes well until the year when there is a terrible drought and nothing grows very well. The day comes for the islanders to hand over the rent to the messenger. What can they do? How will The Owner react?

Age group	6–10 years
Curriculum area focus	**Geography** Using geographical vocabulary. Making maps and plans. Identifying and describing what places are like. Recognising changes in physical and human features – drought. **Mathematics** Counting. Proportions, fractions and percentages (older children).
Speaking and listening	Choosing words with precision. Organising what they say. Including relevant detail. Taking into account the needs of listeners. Using language and actions to explore and convey situations, characters and emotions.

> Creating and sustaining roles.
> Dealing politely with opposing views.

PSHE and Citizenship

What is fair and unfair, right and wrong.
Sharing opinions on things that matter.
Problem solving.
Helping others.
Collaborative work.

Resources

Felt pens, large paper.
Optional props for the messenger: scroll or a large book of accounts.
Optional props for The Owner: cloak.
A large map of the island which can be prepared in advance. This map should be divided into as many pieces as there are going to be small groups of children in the class (see Figure 8.1).

Notes

1. This drama engages the children as one group throughout.
2. The teacher takes two roles: the messenger and The Owner.
3. The drama can be used with a wide age range of children. It seems to have a universal appeal. The responses, reactions and the development of ideas will vary according to age and maturity. The numeracy tasks and the additional possibilities offer opportunities for differentiation according to age or ability.
4. The final outcome of the whole drama is determined by the teacher and the children working together.

Drama activities

1. Building belief in the island community (10 minutes)

[Storytelling; discussion]
Introduce the drama by telling the children that the story is going to take place on an isolated island. Tell the beginning of the story:

> *Long ago and far away on the island of Molagro there was a village. In this village there lived some very hardworking people. The people in the village were farmers. They had to grow everything they ate.*

Discuss this with the children:

> *What do we know so far?*

> *Where is the story set?*

Who are we going to be in the story?

What do we know about the people of Molagro?

2. What does the island look like? (20 minutes)

[Map making]
Discuss what the island will look like. What geographical features will there be? Hills, rivers, forests? Decide on the climate and, importantly, the crops that are grown. Make a list if you like.

Give small groups of children a piece of the island map to draw. Some main features will have already been drawn onto the map to help (see Figure 8.1).

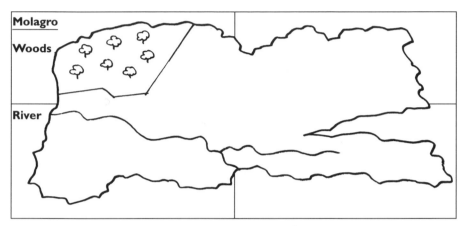

Figure 8.1 A partially completed map of the island

Additional activity
Details of the map-making task can vary according to the age of the children. Older children could take a longer time and refer to maps to see how to signify different features such as lake, marshes, highest point. They could be given a specific number of features to select and include. Here, there is the additional task of interpreting the other groups' parts of the map and their particular features.

Discuss the finished map of the island. What further information do we have about the island now that we have made the map?

3. Introducing the idea of The Owner of the island (15 minutes)

[Storytelling; role on the wall]

There is one building not marked on the map. It is the house where The Owner of the island lives... (Draw or stick a picture of The Owner's house onto the map in a strategic position)... The people have never seen The Owner. The Owner lives a very quiet life in the big house behind the high walls. The Owner never comes out. The Owner never comes to the village. The Owner is very mysterious but the people are very grateful that The Owner lets them use the land to grow crops.

Every year the people of the village must give some of their crops to The Owner as payment for using the land. The Owner's messenger tells the people how much they have to pay each year. Some years it is one hundred bags, some years two hundred. The messenger is the only person on the island who sees The Owner but will not tell the people anything.

We generally keep The Owner gender neutral. Gather together the information they have learned about The Owner so far with a simple role on the wall.

What do we know about The Owner so far?

On to a large piece of paper draw the figure of a person (a stick figure is good – neither male nor female). Write any facts that are known about The Owner in one colour pen. What do we think the people of the village might say about The Owner? Write these things in a different colour pen.

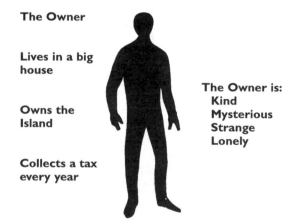

Figure 8.2 Collecting information about The Owner (on the left, known facts written in one colour pen; on the right, villagers' opinions written in another colour)

4. What is the village like? (10 minutes)

[Discussion]
Lead a discussion about the village where everyone lives.

What are the houses like?

Does everyone work on the land?

What kinds of jobs will they do each day?

What would they have to do to harvest the crop?

You may wish to list the jobs that would need to be done – cutting / digging / picking, washing / piling up / putting into bags / carrying the bags, and so on.

5. What do you do in the village? (5 minutes)

[Discussion]
Ask the children to choose what jobs they are going to have in the village at harvest time. They can work individually, in pairs or family groups.

6. It's harvest time in the village (10 minutes)

[Still image and questioning; mime]
Ask the children to set up the harvest scene in the fields outside the village as a moment frozen in time, a still image. Perhaps clarify what they need to remember about making images. Give the children a few minutes to decide what they are going to be doing and where and how they will stand, sit or kneel in the space designated as the field. Give an agreed signal such as 'freeze'. Go round and ask individuals questions about what they are doing that day to help with the harvest.

Tell the children that the image of the people working in the field will be brought to life and they will be able to mime the job that they have chosen. On a given signal, the village is brought to life. This can be stopped at any time using the agreed signal 'freeze!' Teacher can join in the mime, helping with jobs.

7. The harvest is finished (15 minutes)

[Narration; improvisation]
Teacher continues the narration:

It had been a good year. The sun had warmed the ground and the rain had watered the crops. There had been a good harvest; the sacks were filled to the brim. This was the last day of the harvest and all of the villagers were helping with the final few jobs before The Owner's messenger arrived.

Tell the children that they will now be able to add sound to their mimes.

Start with the still image as before and then bring it to life again. This time the mime will have sound added – the villagers can talk to one another and interact. Teacher goes around chatting to the villagers asking about their work, chivvying the workers along and adding detail to the story through conversations with the villagers.

Have you had a busy day?

Are there many more sacks to bring?

Is that very heavy?

I wonder how many sacks the servant will want this year?

We've had a really good harvest this year!

What are you doing today to help with the harvest?

Are you using any tools?

Is the work easy or hard?

How long do you think the work will take?

Do you always do this job or have you done anything else?

What do you think about giving so much of your crop to The Owner?

Have you ever seen The Owner?

8. The messenger comes to collect the tax (15 minutes)

[Teacher in role; ritual]
Tell the children that in the next part of the story you will be the messenger who has been sent by The Owner to collect the tax. Ask the children where the villagers would be waiting to meet the messenger. Tell the children to sit or stand as they decide is appropriate.

Put on a cloak or carry a prop such as a scroll or an important-looking book. Walk slowly towards the villagers. Stand to address them.

> *Thank you for coming to meet me today. This is the last day of the harvest and therefore a very special day for all of us. I am The Owner's servant. Many of you have seen me before. As you know I come here every year to collect the tax that you must pay for the use of this land. You have all worked very hard this year and have had a good harvest. The Owner says that this year three hundred sacks will be a fair amount for you to pay. The sacks will be collected tomorrow. Will each person please bring one sack forward to put in the pile to show their thanks to The Owner for the great kindness that has been shown to you.*

Tell the children that this is a special solemn moment. They will stand in a circle and 'carry' one sack into the middle. They should try to think of some words of thanks to speak, or reveal their thoughts about the event. It should be clear by the way they say the words whether they are spoken (to the messenger) or thoughts (said as a quiet aside).

Thank you for letting us use your land.

There has been a good harvest.

You are very kind.

Three hundred sacks are too many.

I wonder what The Owner is like?

We've had a good harvest this year so I suppose it's okay for The Owner to ask for so much.

9. The villagers plan for next year (30 minutes): optional mathematics activity

[Narration; mathematics]

The villagers started thinking about how they farmed the land. They discussed ways that may enable them to produce more so that everyone could have a little extra over the long cold winter.

They also discussed how much The Owner would ask for next year. They never knew what to expect. For the first time the villagers considered their harvest over the last few years and what The Owner had asked for.

The scene is set to create a context in which important calculations are required of the villagers. For younger children this may involve tallying and counting activities. Select the number of bags appropriate to the mathematical abilities of the children you are working with. A simple example is:

- This year we produced 30 bags and gave The Owner 3.
  How many did we have left?
  Last year we produced 40 bags and gave The Owner 4.
  How many did we have left?

Older children can consider proportions, fractions and percentages. Again the number of bags should be appropriate for the abilities of the children. In the following example the children will discover that The Owner takes 10 per cent of the crop.

This year we produced   3000 bags. We gave The Owner   300 bags.
Last year we produced   1600 bags. We gave The Owner   160 bags.
The year before it was   3520 bags. We gave The Owner   352 bags.

You may choose any percentage that will challenge your children. You may prefer to use fractions.

Why does The Owner ask for different amounts each year?

What proportion have we had to give in the different years?

Does the proportion vary?

What does The Owner get as a fraction of our crop?

Is the percentage that is taken consistent from one year to the next?

Children do the calculations above and below.

The villagers decided to work out how they could make the most of the land they were allowed to farm, and to calculate what the owner would take next year.

If we have a very good year: 3600 bags.
   The Owner will take … (360).
If we leave two fields fallow: 2800 bags.
   The Owner will take … (280).
If we use more fertiliser: 4400 bags.
   The Owner will take … (440).

You can build on these ideas and create many other mathematical calculations. The children as villagers can make up their own production possibilities.

10. The next year is not so good (15 minutes)

[Storytelling; still images with questions and thought tap]

The following year the villagers worked very, very hard and dreamed of a bumper crop. However, it was not a good year. The rains did not come. The earth dried up in the sun. The crops would not grow. The rivers, streams and wells all dried up. There was a terrible drought. The people were hungry. Some were ill. It was a bad time.

Ask the children to work in small groups to make still images of the village this year. View the images in turn. Tap the villagers on their shoulders and ask what they are thinking or what is happening to them.

What has happened this year?

Has there been any rain?

What has happened to the crop?

Where are you getting water to drink?

Is there much water left in the village?

Isn't the messenger due to be arriving to collect the tax today?

What will you do this year if you have nothing to give?

11. The messenger arrives again (5 minutes)

[Teacher in role]
In role as the messenger, meet the villagers as before. Ask them for

one hundred sacks this year. Obviously a discussion will develop. Below are some of the arguments on both sides that usually crop up. Arguments of the messenger:

Sorry to hear the bad news but this is unacceptable.

If you can't pay then you will have to leave the island.

The Owner must have the tax.

That is the agreement.

I can't go back without the tax. I wouldn't dare.

Arguments of the villagers:

There is nothing to give this time because of the drought.

Our people are hungry.

The Owner must understand these circumstances.

If we give, we die.

We have always given before.

Say that you will wait while they decide what they are going to do. Walk away and put down any props. Run back to the group and gather them around you as if you were one of the islanders.

12. What can the villagers do? (10 minutes)

[Meeting]
Lead a debate about what could be done. What are the possibilities?

What shall we do?

We can't pay anything!

Surely The Owner must know what a terrible time we've been having.

Does The Owner realise how difficult it has been for us?

The messenger seems to be too scared to go and tell The Owner.

Would it be a good idea if we went to The Owner's house to tell our story? The Owner must listen to us.

This meeting might lead the children to different conclusions. Usually they want to speak to The Owner. Other possibilities that might be discussed are writing a letter to The Owner explaining the situation, or deciding to leave the island.

13. Arriving at The Owner's house (10 minutes)

[Collective storytelling]
The messenger tells the villagers that they must go to The Owner's house in an hour for a meeting.

The description of the house can be created through collective storytelling. In this approach the teacher begins sentences and invites children to finish them off with their own ideas about what will be appropriate.

The teacher's storytelling will obviously reflect the age of the children. Younger children may be asked to comment on colours while older children may describe the atmosphere.

> *The villagers arrived at The Owner's house and waited. The outside of the house looked..... the doorway was..... The atmosphere was..... After a while the door slowly opened and they were invited to come in. As they walked into the hall they were amazed at what they saw. The house was really..... (could be huge, beautiful, full of expensive ornaments, or dark, spooky, dirty, smelly, and so on), the walls were .....(could be slimy, covered in expensive paintings or painted blue and so on), the curtains were..... and the floor was.....*

14. Meeting The Owner (10–15 minutes)

[Teacher in role and meeting]
Ask the children what they are expecting The Owner to be like. Tell the children that in the next part of the drama you will be The Owner.

The meeting of the villagers with The Owner can take many directions. It is interesting to allow the children to consider what The Owner might be like. They could possibly suggest that The Owner is, in fact, feeble, pathetic and has no real power over them, being easily persuaded to forget the tax this year (and every other year maybe). They may imagine that The Owner could be as frightening as expected, and will not accept their explanations and force them all to leave the island.

Of course, The Owner may turn out to be a mixture of both. This is up to the teacher! It may depend on the effectiveness of the children's persuasion.

Possible lines of argument for The Owner:

> *Do you think you can live on my island and not pay me?*

> *You have to feed yourselves, so do I.*

> *You have always accepted that a portion/a tenth/10 per cent (depending on the age of the children) is a fair amount.*

> *I see no reason why I should not have what is owed to me.*

> *I don't give you any trouble or hurt you in any way.*

> *I am a fair person.*

Lines of argument for the villagers that we have heard:

We are ill.

We will die.

This year is different.

Rules aren't made of gold. They don't have to last forever when they don't work.

You must be fair to us.

Do you want us to die?

If we die you won't get anything.

Can't we come to an agreement about this?

You can decide whether The Owner relents, compromises, agrees or refuses to give in.

15. Reflecting on the drama (5 minutes)

Discuss the outcome of the meeting between The Owner and the villagers. Was it as expected? What kind of person did The Owner turn out to be? What will happen in the future?

1. Writing from the perspective of a villager
   Different villagers' viewpoints could be considered through writing their story in role.
   Personal diaries and letters are other options for writing in role.
2. Individual or shared letter writing
   A letter can be written to The Owner either thanking or complaining about the decision made.
3. Prediction
   What happened next could be discussed in small groups or as a class. Alternatively a paragraph to tell the next part of the story can be written or enacted in small groups.
4. Character description
   Younger or less able children could choose words to describe The Owner. Older or more able children could list adjectives and adverbs in preparation for writing a character description. (They could be given a model from literature to use.)

Additional possibilities

Chapter 9

King Lear
A classic text

The children first create an imagined community in Lear's kingdom. They hear the news that their beloved King is to retire and hand over his kingdom to his daughters. Everyone knows that there is only one nice daughter, Cordelia. As loyal subjects the children hear Lear announce that he will give land to his daughters according to how much they say they love him. Cordelia cannot do this, although she loves her father very much. She is banished. The children consider this decision and its consequences.

Age group	8–11 years
Curriculum area focus	**English** Shakespeare play. Understanding and appreciating literary text. Learning about character. Looking for meaning beyond the literal. Responding imaginatively to classic text.
Speaking and listening	Adapting speech for a range of purposes and audiences. Asking relevant questions to develop ideas. Listening, understanding and responding to others. Dealing politely with opposing views.
PSHE and Citizenship	Awareness of different kinds of responsibilities. Using imagination to understand other people's responsibilities.

Empathy – realising that our actions affect ourselves and others, caring about other people's feelings, and trying to see things from their point of view.

Resources

Pieces of paper with the three quotations and questions written on them (activity 9).
A cloak for the King (optional).

Time

This extended exploration could be spread over a few days or even weeks. These activities could take approximately three and a half to four hours.

1. Given the importance of Shakespeare in the National Curriculum, it is important that children have a positive experience of his work. This drama looks at the beginning of *King Lear*, focusing only on Lear's family story and not Gloucester's.
2. You do not need to know the play to teach it because everything you need is provided for you. Some extracts to be read to the children in the drama are provided. They are not direct quotations, though there is a feel of the text through the inclusion of certain phrases. At one stage in the drama, the children deal directly with snippets of text.
3. Our experience is that this work gives children pleasure in terms of both the story and the intriguing language, and therefore generates a positive attitude towards Shakespeare.

1. Establishing the characters (10 minutes)

[Game]
This is played like the game Fruit Salad. In a circle of chairs, each child is allocated one of the following trades: blacksmith, baker, potter; the group word is Albion. (Children do not yet need to know that this is the old word for England used in the play.)

One child in the centre calls either a trade or the word Albion. If 'potter' is called, then all potters must leave their chairs, and run to other chairs and the child in the centre aims to run to sit in an empty chair. The same for the other trades. If Albion is called, the children have to leave their chairs for different ones. Each time, the child who fails to get a seat is the next one to call from the centre.

2. Introducing who, when and where in King Lear (10 minutes)

[Teacher reading]
Remember to vary the voice, look at individual listeners and use some gestures because it is a long introduction.

> *Once upon a time there was an old King who ruled the land called Albion. This King had three daughters, Goneril, Regan and, the youngest, Cordelia. The people of Albion knew the King to be an old proud man, and although they knew his faults, they were happy that during his reign there had been no wars. The reign of King Lear was coming to an end, for the king was growing old. The people knew that between his daughters there was little love, and they feared that when the old King passed away the thinly disguised mistrust might break out into open war.*

> *Goneril was the eldest of King Lear's daughters. She loved her father because he was the king, and not to do so would be dangerous. Regan was Lear's second daughter. She loved her father because of what she might gain from him. Cordelia was the third. She loved her father simply because he was her father.*

> *Lear was King to all three, but a father to one, Cordelia. Now the people knew that it was wrong for the King to have a favourite, but no one knew whether it was because she was his favourite that she loved him more, or because she loved him more that she became his favourite. The fact was that he loved her most and she loved him dearly. Goneril and Regan knew this, the people of Albion knew this.*

> *In truth Cordelia was the people's favourite, for they feared the cunning of Goneril and the cruelty of Regan. With Cordelia they knew, as with the King, that they would be safe.*

Invite the children in turn to say anything that they have learned about the characters in the story to check and confirm their comprehension.

3. The community's views are heard (20 minutes)

[Questioning the roles; pairwork; discussion in role]
To help the children imagine their roles, ask them questions. Speak to the children as villagers, drawing on the trades from the initial game.

> *Aren't you a blacksmith? You must know something about that Goneril because she has many horses... What have you heard about her?*

> *Do you bake bread for the King and his family?... What do you think of your King? I've heard everyone thinks he's fair.*

In pairs children tell each other stories about their experiences of the royal family. Some will be bad – for instance, the blacksmith who saw Goneril using spurs on a horse to the extent that the horse was bleeding; and some will be good – such as Cordelia's kindness to a sick child in the village.

Bring the children together in a group and ask to hear their experiences. Help to create the atmosphere by nodding or looking horrified, or whatever, when appropriate.

4. An invitation to King Lear's Great Hall (15 minutes)

[Improvisation; narration]
The children create their village to help them build belief in the fiction. To help their imaginations they could use some props, such as tables as baker's counters. The teacher wanders around them extending their dramatic play through interacting as a villager.

May I buy some bread?

Do you serve hot food?

You've lived in this village all your life, haven't you?

How is your son? Wasn't he poorly?

Do you do the deliveries of bread to the king?

Have you seen Cordelia about recently?

Ask the children to freeze their positions at work. Now narrate:

It was on the first day of winter, at the setting of the sun, that the people received the King's most loyal and trusted servant, Kent. The Earl of Kent was no ordinary messenger, so the people knew immediately that whatever was about to happen was very important. Kent read an announcement: 'People of Albion. The King requests you to attend his palace, tomorrow. On the stroke of the eleventh hour you are to put down your work and meet in the Great Hall.'

5. Thoughts on why the invitation came and what will happen (5 minutes)

[Discussion in role]
Teacher explains that all the villagers gathered by the fire in the central square that night to discuss why they might have been asked to go to the Great Hall. Teacher takes a role of a villager too, controlling the discussion and asking questions.

What do you think it is all about?

Do you reckon King Lear will actually be there?

What do you think the Great Hall will look like?

Will we hear about our King's retirement?

What will he say? Do you think he has changed his mind?

6. Preparing to greet a King (20 minutes)

[Game; preparing roles]
Explain that they will play Captain's Coming, but with a difference. The teacher calls that someone is coming and the children instantly respond as indicated below:

Captain's coming! (All stand straight and salute)
Friend's coming! (All stand with their palms out and say 'Give me five')
Mum's coming! (All lie down and pretend to be asleep)
King's coming! (All bow or curtsey)

Between the commands the children wander about in a walk appropriate for whoever they have just met: thus they walk upright after the King, they march after the captain. The children may wish to decide on this. They enjoy a 'dudie walk' after meeting the friend!

The last call in the game should be King's coming!

Then place a chair at one end and ask a child to sit as the King. The rest of the children stand in lines at the other end of the room. Explain that when children are tapped on the shoulder they step forward towards the King and bow or curtsey. They can be tapped in pairs and greet the King together to save time.

Discuss what sort of walk would be appropriate:

How fast should we walk?

How should we hold our heads?

What should we look at?

Should we look casual, frightened, dignified, confused?

Teacher calls out advice if necessary.

As they walk back, they should stand forming two lines either side of the King.

7. The scene in the Great Hall (30 minutes)

[Teacher narration; class narration]
The children sit in their lines. Teacher narrates:

The room was set out in a very formal way. The Great Hall was huge. A chair was positioned at the far end of the hall, in the centre..... (teacher places a chair with significance and dignity).....This chair was for the King. To one side and further forward, another smaller chair stood..... (teacher places a second chair).....There was a second smaller chair positioned to the other side of the King's chair, also a little in front..... (this is done slowly and with dignity, making it significant).....A further chair was positioned at a distance in front of the King's chair. Thus three chairs were positioned facing the King's chair but at a respectable distance.

The children take it in turns to describe the Great Hall with the special task of using their voices to create the feel of the space. Each describes the feel or the look of the huge room. For example:

There were rows of huge candles along the walls.

The hall was huge with very high walls.

The walls were stone.

The floors were shiny marble.

It felt very different from my small smelly baker's kitchen.

Finally, narrate using the phrases or ideas the children have given, to fix the atmosphere and to give value to the children's contributions, and for them to hear how good their description sounds.

Continue with the gist of the following (or read it), looking at the imaginary figures described as though you can see them entering and sitting down:

At last, after what seemed like hours, the great door opened and King Lear entered. There was a warmth in the air for his people loved the old King. They knew that, whatever else, he had always been fair. They could see he was tired, they could see he was old.

He walked across to his chair and sat down. Soon after, another figure entered. It was Goneril. She moved over to the first chair nearest the door and she, the eldest of Lear's daughters, sat down. The air in the room seemed to chill as she entered. There was an uncomfortable feel in the Great Hall. All knew how she loved the King because he was the King, not to love him may be dangerous.

Next the second daughter, Regan, entered. Still the room felt hushed. They all looked at her knowing how she loved the King because of what she could gain. There was no warm feeling for her as she moved to the second chair opposite the King.

Finally, the third and youngest sister entered. All felt the rush of warmth and loyalty and all saw the flicker of a smile on the old King's face. Cordelia walked over to the empty chair and sat down.

8. Lear's decision (15 minutes)

[Whole class improvisation and teacher in role]
Explain that they will now need to take shared roles as the three sisters to continue the meeting in the Great Hall. One trade (potter, baker or blacksmith) group is needed for each sister. Tell them to enter the Great Hall as before, bow to the King (teacher in role) then take their positions in an arc behind the appropriate sister's chair.

The King then rises and reads/says:

Meantime we shall express our darker purpose. Give me the map. Princes, nobles, and villagers of Albion know that it is our intention on this day to give the rule of this kingdom to those who are younger; I have grown old and it is time for younger strengths and minds to govern the land and the people of all our villages. Therefore we will divide our kingdom between our three daughters, Goneril, Regan and Cordelia.

But which of you deserves the most? Which of you can say you love your father the most, and by doing so win a larger, richer part of our kingdom? Goneril, the eldest, speak first. How much do you love your father?

At this point, teacher stands and takes the cloak off and replaces it on the chair/throne.
Speak to the children as teacher to check that they have understood what was said.

Why is he handing over his kingdom?

How is he going to divide up his kingdom?

What has he asked the daughters?

What do you think they will say?

9. The sisters reply (45 minutes)

[Shared group roles; teacher in role; whole class improvisation]
Explain that the King will ask Goneril, Regan and finally Cordelia. Each group must prepare their reply to the King's question. They are given some lines to help them and around which to base their response. The children will take it in turns to be the voice of their character, sitting behind her chair. The groups will need time to:

- make sense of their lines;
- discuss what else might be said;
- agree on the order and who says what.

The given lines are placed on each daughter's chair. Each group see only their own character's lines.

Group 1:
Goneril – *'Sir, I love you more than words can wield the matter'*.

Group 2:
Regan – *'she names my very deed of love; Only she comes too short'*.

Group 3:
Cordelia – *'Unhappy that I am, I cannot heave My heart into my mouth.....Nothing, my lord'*.

Each group will need some help to make sense of their lines. It is helpful to provide an A4 card for each group with the appropriate quotation and some of the questions posed below. The groups can then begin their discussions on their own.

Group 1:

What do we know about Goneril?

What is she likely to say to the King when asked this question?

Might she lie and go over the top about her love for him?

Cover the last three words of the quotation and ask them to read it and think what we might say next: 'than words can...say.' They then have the meaning of the line. They make up what else she could say, perhaps 'You mean more to me than anything in the world'.

Group 2:

What do we know about Regan?

What is she likely to say?

What does the quotation mean?

What might Regan add to what Goneril has said?

Group 3:

What do you think the youngest sister will say?

What do you think Cordelia would think about Goneril and Regan and what they say?

What do we associate with heart? (feelings, love)

What do we associate with mouth? (words, talking)

What might Cordelia mean and why is she unhappy?

Why does she say 'nothing' and what can't she explain?

Why doesn't she want to explain it in front of all the gathered people?

All now return to their formal positions in the Great Hall with teacher in role as Lear on his throne.

Return to the point where the King asks the question of Goneril.

Goneril, the eldest, speak first. How much do you love your father?

Group 1 answer as planned. The King then turns to Regan and Group 2 answer. Finally, he turns to Cordelia. The King may try to persuade her to speak of her love, but eventually threatens her, telling her that if she says nothing she will not get a third of his kingdom. When the King eventually tells her that she is banished from the kingdom, never to return to the soil of Albion, you will sense the shock of all the children. However, in role as the sisters they are not in a position to say anything. The King leaves the Great Hall.

10. Lear's best friend intervenes (15 minutes)

[Discussion, corporate role and teacher in role]
Teacher asks the children what they think about what happened in the Great Hall. (When we first ran this drama, we were not going to include Kent's advice, but the children were desperate to tell Lear that Cordelia loves him and that he was making a big mistake.) This activity gives them a way of speaking to the King. Explain that someone else felt exactly as they do.

Do you remember the name of the very special friend of the King?

They heard of him in activity 4: Kent. The Earl of Kent brought them the message from the King to attend the palace. The children now can speak as Kent, the King's loyal and trusted servant.

Teacher sits on the throne in role as Lear and asks why Kent is so keen to speak. The children take it in turns in the order in which they are seated to stand up and speak as Kent. If any of them don't wish to do so, they remain seated and the next child stands.

Lear will not hear of any criticism of either himself or of the two older daughters. He warns of the danger of suggesting that he is foolish. Finally, when all have had their say and tried to explain, Lear shocks them again by banishing Kent from Albion, too.

11. Sleepless Lear thinks about the day (15 minutes)

[Sculpting; thought tracking]
Tell the children that Lear had a terrible night's sleep. He couldn't stop thinking about everything that had been said. He could hardly believe that he had banished his favourite daughter and his best friend.

Ask them to consider how he was sitting in his room. One chair is placed in the centre and a volunteer sits on it as Lear. The children are asked to make suggestions about how he might be sitting. The volunteer tries out positions suggested by the rest of the class – head in hands, and so on – and finally selects a position.

They now consider what he might be thinking.

What have I done?

Does she really not love me?

There was something in Goneril's eye that frightens me.

Lear remains in the chair frozen. One by one the others move into a space around Lear and speak aloud in an appropriate voice what he might be thinking. They should then freeze in a position that suits what has been said. They could look up, curl on the floor with pain, rub their hands together, hold head in hands, or lie face down with their fists clenched in frustration.

This will continue until everyone is frozen around Lear. You may wish to move between them and touch them gently on the shoulder to hear their thoughts again. This enhances a seriousness because they are in the posture and are less aware of others looking on.

12. Creating endings (10–30 minutes)

This is, of course, only the first part of Shakespeare's *King Lear*. It has introduced characters, a good story and a sense of the language. Shakespeare took the story from a familiar tale which also tells of the cruelty of Goneril and Regan. Lear, having learnt from his mistake, is happily reunited with Cordelia and Kent. However, Shakespeare deprived us of a happy ending.

Children may choose an ending for the story to follow activity 11. The ending could be explored in various ways:

- Story circle: the children sit in a circle and take it in turns to say a sentence until they have concluded the story.
- Still images: small groups agree an ending and create four still images to tell it.
- Written endings: different written tasks need to be given to different age groups and/or abilities.

1. Teacher led discussion
   Look at Shakespeare's ending.
2. Individual writing
   Write a letter from Cordelia to her father, after she has been banished.
3. Reading
   Look at Act 1 Scene 1 from the line: 'Meantime, we shall express our darker purpose.' Volunteers may read the script aloud.

Additional possibilities

Chapter 10

The Romans in Britain
History

The children in role as time travellers discover details of the Roman attack on Anglesey in AD 60. The all-powerful 'Great Mistress of Time' has a mission for the new team of travellers. They must go into the past and report on what they discover. They meet people from the past and get involved in past events, learning about the Roman occupation and the Britons' various responses to it. The children move between roles in the past and their time travelling roles in the present. They must therefore address the situation from the point of view of the Romans, and of the Britons, as well as of observers in the present.

Age group	8–11 years
Curriculum area focus	**History** Romans in Britain: Knowledge and understanding of events, people and changes in the past, 'the ideas, beliefs, attitudes and experiences of men and women and children in the past'. Historical interpretation: 'to recognise that the past is represented and interpreted in different ways, and to give reasons for this.' Organisation and communication: 'to communicate their knowledge and understanding in a variety of ways.' World history study: the effects of Roman settlement.
Speaking and listening	Adapting speech for a range of different purposes. Taking up and sustaining different roles, adapting them to suit the situation.

Asking relevant questions to clarify.
Extending and following up ideas.
Recalling and re-presenting important
features of an argument.
Responding to others appropriately,
taking into account what they say.

PSHE and Citizenship Considering different viewpoints,
cultural differences.
Thinking about the lives of people
living in other places and times, and
people with different values and
customs.
Recognising difference and
challenging stereotypes.

Resources Felt pens, large sheets of paper.
Time travel task provided (see Figure
10.1).

Time These activities will take different
lengths of time with different groups
depending on the nature of the
responses. Overall, this work will take
most groups between two and a half
and three hours.

1. This lesson provides a structure we call 'The Time Machine' that can be used for lots of different historical contexts. We have used it for Victorians, and Ancient Greece too. It provides the opportunity to give enormous amounts of information in the drama and to consider critically.
2. This drama involves whole group drama and small group activities.
3. The teacher takes three roles: the Time Travel Controller; Marcus, a young Roman soldier; and an old Druid. It is possible to remain in role working with the children in the drama for long periods of time, without needing to address them as teacher in between different parts of the drama. However, you may prefer to do one mission into the past at a time and follow each up with some written tasks. These activities can be done over a couple of weeks, days, or in one go. You may wish to do only the first meeting, with Marcus the Roman soldier.
4. Historical information required for the drama is provided at the end of the lesson.

Notes

Drama activities

1. Let's talk about time travel stories (5 minutes)

[Discussion]
Introduce the session by leading a general discussion about familiar books, television programmes and films about time travel.

Which have you read / seen?

How does Dr Who move in time?

What makes the films or books convincing?

Do they take people forward or back in time?

2. Setting the scene (5 minutes)

[Defining space and setting the scene]
Tell the class that they are going to be involved in a drama about time travellers. Arrange the class in a circle on chairs and give the outline of the following:

When you are sitting on your chairs, you are in role as time travellers in the present day. However, everything that takes place in the centre of the circle is taking place in the time tunnel, and therefore in the past or future. It is through the time tunnel that moments of other times can be viewed.

We are all in the drama when I am inside our circle of chairs, but when I step behind my chair, it is the sign that I am out of role and will speak to you as your teacher.

Are you ready for the time travel drama?

3. Children meet the Time Travel Controller (5 minutes)

[Teacher in role; ritual]
Take the role of the Time Travel Controller, who shows a deep reverence for the Great Mistress of Time who is in charge of the time machine. She is never seen, but her requests and comments are passed to the time travellers through you, the controller.

Welcome them all and explain that before they are permitted to hear any details of the Time Machine Missions they are required by the Great Mistress of Time to swear an oath. They must stand and raise their right hand.

Raise your right arm, with palm facing down, hand straight towards the centre of the circle. This should be done as though it is of crucial importance with a serious expression. When all the children have their right hands out, ask them to repeat the oath together after you:

I swear

to keep the secrets

of the time machine.

Ask the children to be seated.

4. Introducing the task (5 minutes)

[Teacher in role]
Set out the first task:

> *A little while ago, the Great Mistress of Time programmed the time machine for North Wales AD 60. She observed a young man talking to himself. What she saw made her feel very concerned and so she would like you to find out more for her. She has asked that I read you her account of what she saw.*

This is provided in Figure 10.1. It looks best if you read it from a photocopied sheet, rather than from this book.

5. Preparing to meet the Roman soldier (10 minutes)

[In role discussion]

> *Time travellers, it is the request of the Great Mistress of Time that we programme the machine to North Wales AD 60 and find this young man. We will then have to ask him questions to find out as much as we can about him and his life. What sort of questions might we ask?*

They may like to discuss in time travel pairs first. Expect questions such as:

> *What is your name?*
>
> *Why are you crying?*
>
> *How old are you?*
>
> *What are the sharp things beside you?*
>
> *Why are you wearing such odd clothes?*

Ask them if they are ready for their mission, reminding them that the Mistress will want a very full report.

6. First mission in time: Marcus (10–45 minutes)

[Class improvisation]
Teacher in role stands up as the time traveller in serious mode. Mime turning dials and pushing buttons as you say the following:

AD 60   North Wales

I saw a man weeping. He looked young, strong and healthy. He was quite alone.

There were strange objects beside him, but I couldn't make out what they were. Something looked sharp. His clothes were strange – made of metal, I think.
I wondered if he was uncomfortable in the outfit.

He was muttering but I couldn't make out what he said. I'm sure I heard, between the sobs,
'Numbers against magic'.
I wonder what he meant.
He also said,
'So far, too far', about something.

Figure 10.1   The account from the Great Mistress of Time

I wish you well. I am not permitted to accompany you on this, your first mission. I will programme the machine and soon a vision of this young man in the past will appear before your eyes…in the tunnel of time.

Find out all you can. The Great Mistress of Time needs to know everything.

Turn slowly in circles, moving into the centre of the circle. Sit down in the middle to become Marcus, a young Roman soldier, wiping his eyes. Marcus is innocent and friendly. He means well and will gain the children's affection. He is excited about the weapons, yet worried about their consequences. He believes that he is doing what is right. The class as time travellers question Marcus, who is happy to have someone to speak to. Here an enormous amount of information can be given. Details can be found in background information at the end of this chapter.

Marcus shows off his two javelins and short sword, proud that it is not long and unwieldy like the Britons' swords. He asks them not to be afraid when he shows them his helmet on his head, because it is designed to frighten off the enemy. He explains how he has been trained to march, to use his shield, and how the Britons fight.

In response to questions about his tears, he may deny them at first. His fear is of the battle he is forced to fight the next day. He believes that the Druids are magic and may therefore overwhelm even the best trained soldiers. He tells that the Druids are evil since they make human sacrifices in the forest. The Britons have not been grateful for all that the Romans have brought to Britain. They didn't have roads or cities before, and in return they are fighting! Some have been very nice and made friends with Roman generals, but not the Druids on Anglesey. Marcus misses his family. He is only 14-years-old. He is proud of being a soldier, but is afraid and needs reassurance that he will be all right. Finally, he explains that he must get back to the camp or he will be missed by his best friend Phillipos.

Stand and turn slowly in circles moving back towards the Time Travel Controller's chair. Sit on it and then look up as the Time Travel Controller.

7. Reporting back on the findings (10 minutes)

[Role on the wall]
As Time Travel Controller, ask the time travellers if they saw anyone. What did they find out?

The time travellers are introduced to the way that all missions in the time tunnel are recorded. A large sheet of paper is spread onto the floor. Draw a stick figure to represent Marcus and write around it as much information provided by Marcus as the children can remember. Write the information in note form as it is offered by the children. It can be about the Romans' fighting techniques, the

Druids, and Marcus himself. You could write details of Britons and Romans in different colours (see Figure 10.2).

His name is Marcus.

He is frightened of the Druids.

The Romans all carry two javelins each.

You, as the time traveller, were not on the mission with the children, so you can use the role to clarify details, thus:

Did he tell you the name of the island the Druids were on?

What did his helmet look like?

What were the sharp things?

MARCUS

Figure 10.2 Marcus: role on the wall

And you can also challenge the information:

Did he ever actually see the Druids doing magic?

Did he think that the Britons wanted new roads?

Avoid correcting information (perhaps the number of javelins), because in the drama, you weren't there! Usually the children correct one another at this stage, otherwise you can give correct information later in the drama.

When all the information they have is noted on the paper, congratulate the team on their first mission.

8. The Roman soldiers prepare (10 minutes)

[Class improvisation and teacher in role]
Move outside the circle of chairs and, speaking as teacher, explain that the children will soon need to become people in the past for the next part of the drama.

Back inside the circle, the Time Travel Controller passes on the Mistress's interest in their work and in the life of Marcus. They are now to travel back in time to the same place, but this time to the following morning to see what happened next.

They are to be introduced to the 'freeze control' facility of the time machine that stops any given moment in time so that it can be examined.

As I programme the time machine (mime turning dials as before) an image will appear. I can see a scene as the swirling mists clear. It is early morning. I can see a cold grey sea (point). On the beach there are rows of soldiers standing very upright, in silence. They stand in rows facing the sea.

Indicate to the children that they are to become the soldiers.

They must be waiting for something very important…oh, yes, there is a general coming to speak to them!

Step in front of the rows and address the soldiers as their general. Now is the opportunity to correct any misinformation from the first mission. Perhaps they didn't catch the name of the island, for example. Through this role you can also give additional information. Tell them:

- it is to be a very important battle today;
- the Druids must be destroyed because they have resisted the Romans;
- the Druids still make human sacrifices, which Romans stopped long ago;
- to remember all their training – javelins thrown only on command, shields above them, close together to protect from arrows and spears, and so on;

- they will cross the Menai Straits to the island of Anglesey in flat bottomed boats;
- mounted soldiers will swim across with their horses;
- Druids must be killed to make Britain a safer place;
- the wood on Anglesey must be cut down because the Druids believe it is sacred and make their sacrifices there.

Ask if there are any questions.

9. Freeze control and soldiers thoughts (5 minutes)

[Still image and thought tap]
Return to the edge of the circle and explain that you are going to turn on the freeze control now, which will freeze this moment in time.

Walking around the still image of soldiers you wonder what they are thinking. A new device on the time machine can enable you to tap soldiers on the shoulder and they speak aloud their thoughts. Provide some examples.

Perhaps one is thinking, 'I am afraid', or 'Are the Druids really magic?' or maybe, 'I wish I was at home'.

Tap individuals and hear the thoughts. You may need to repeat each one so that they are all heard.

Finally, return to your position as Time Travel Controller.

The image is slowly and silently fading away.

Gesture to the children to return to their time travel seats.

10. Reporting back new information (5–10 minutes)

[Role on the wall]
A report must be made of the second mission for the Great Mistress of Time. Revisit the Marcus role on the wall and add new information or correct anything that was recorded wrongly. Alternatively, you could use a new sheet for the second mission. This time you can comment on what was observed because you were watching events through the time tunnel, too.

11. Meanwhile, on Anglesey (10 minutes)

[Teacher in role]
The time travellers are told that the Great Mistress of Time is curious to know how the other side is preparing on Anglesey. Their next mission will take them over the Menai Straits. A full report will again be requested.

The controls are set. Looking into the time tunnel, describe the vision revealed:

There are crowds of people sitting down on the ground, all facing the sea. (Gesture for the children to sit as the Britons.) The women are all clad in black and the Druid priests are looking fearfully out to sea and to the heavens. It's a cold day and many are hugging themselves to keep warm. No one speaks. At last someone gets to his feet. He is an old man with a wise though anxious face. All turn with respect to listen to him.

Stand and give the gist or read the old Druid's speech.

We know the gods are on our side. The gods know that this is our land. These intruders have no right to walk on our land, no right to shed our blood, no right to interfere with our sacred ways. All of us here know how they have persuaded many Britons, with money and honours, to lay down their swords.

I am proud that I am here with Britons who will not be bought or threatened by Roman invaders. We wish to keep our soil for those of future generations. We do not wish to have their new cities, we like things as they were.

Let us be true to ourselves and the gods and fight with all our might. We will wait here until they come, then run at them with swords, clubs and anything we have, shouting curses upon those who wish to destroy what means so much to us.

Thank you. I honour you for your courage.

---

12. What the Britons say about the Romans (15 minutes)

[Overheard conversations]
Step outside the chairs to give instructions as teacher.

Explain that the Britons talked, as they waited, about all that had been said and about their hopes and fears. Ask the children to chat with those near them in threes or fours as though they are the Britons. When you clap your hands it is the freeze control and they must remain still. You will then wander about the groups. When you stand by a group, they must continue their conversation until you move on.

When conversations have been heard, end the mission by describing the image slowly disappearing and gesturing to the children to return to their seats.

13. Reporting back (5–10 minutes)

[Role on the wall]
Draw up a new report on a sheet of paper with the outline shape of an island drawn in the middle.

What did you see happening on Anglesey?

Did they look ready for the battle?

Why were they fighting against good people, anyway?

What did they talk about?

Were they like you thought they would be?

14. Photographs of the battle (20 minutes)

[Small group still images]
The Time Travel Controller informs the time travellers that the Great Mistress of Time is very impressed by their work, and asks if they will complete one final mission. She wants them to watch the battle and take photographs for her of what they see.

As teacher, outside the circle of chairs, explain that in groups of three or four they should create two photographs showing moments of the battle. They must use their new knowledge of how the Romans and Britons fight so that it is clear who is fighting on which side.

As Time Travel Controller, invite each group in turn to show the photographs they have taken. These can be discussed. Then ask for all the photos to be placed in the centre to create a big battle scene.

As teacher, outside the circle, explain that you will narrate the battle story and if they are tapped on the shoulder, they must silently fall to the floor as dead.

Walk slowly between the children's photos as you narrate the battle. Use your voice to create a tense atmosphere as you explain the Romans' initial fear at the sight of the Druids, then describe the huge numbers of well-equipped, trained soldiers moving in on the untrained, ill-equipped Britons. As you move, gradually touch the shoulders of more Britons than Romans to signify deaths. Describe the fighting, the Britons' long swords and the sounds that filled the air, of anguish and weeping.

After destroying most of the Britons, the order was given to cut down the sacred wood.

Mime chopping down trees and then, looking at the children, some remaining in fighting positions and others dead, describe the image of the battle fading, and return to time travel seats.

15. Questions, considerations and implications (20 minutes)

[In role discussion]
The Time Travel Controller congratulates the time travellers. Their work has intrigued, fascinated and bewildered the Great Mistress of Time. She would be very grateful if they would consider some questions:

If you had been alive in AD 60, who would you have rather been?

What exactly were the different views?

Who do you think should have won the battle?

Who do you think was right?

Should the Romans have been in Britain?

Did you feel sympathy for either side? Both?

They are thanked for their work and assured that they are the best team of time travellers ever to take a mission in the time machine.

Additional possibilities

1. Individual writing
   Written reports of every mission could be made so that each child produces a log of what has been discovered.
2. Pair or individual listing task
   Under two columns, entitled Fact and Fiction, children list what happened in their drama that was based on fact – for example, in AD 60 the Romans mounted an attack on Anglesey – and things that were based on fiction – for example, a boy called Marcus who was afraid of fighting. This may raise some interesting discussion about evidence and viewpoint.
3. Individual drawing and labelling
   Draw Marcus, and label the different features of the Roman foot soldier, like the short sword. Provide the specifications and advantages. Children may wish to look up pictures in reference books.
4. Research activities
   Individuals or small groups can be given tasks to find out different aspects of life in Rome. They could be asked to prepare diagrams, or drawings to present their findings to the Time Travel Controller (teacher in role) for the files of the Great Mistress of Time.
5. Map work
   Maps or charts can be drawn to illustrate the journey Marcus had made from Rome to Britain and to North Wales and Anglesey.
6. Whole class assembly
   The class could present their findings to other children at an assembly. They can speak as though they are time travellers reporting on the adventures and discoveries they have made

through a time tunnel. Different small groups can be given different missions to report on. Perhaps the Dr Who theme tune, or other familiar appropriate music could be played at the beginning and end.

Background information

Marcus

Marcus is in the Roman army. He is 14-years-old. He was very sorry to leave his family in Rome, but proud to march with the army as his brothers and father did.

'So far, too far' refers to the long distance he has travelled from warm blue-skied Rome, to cold grey Britian. There are things he misses about home. It was a long tiring march to get here.

Marcus has crept from the soldiers' tent at night to be alone. He is embarrassed by his tears and may pretend that he hasn't been crying. He is afraid because General Suetonius is to give the command tomorrow morning. They must cross the Menai Straits to invade Anglesey.

'Numbers against magic' refers to the Roman soldiers' belief that the Druid priests, who had gathered in Anglesey, had magic powers. Marcus is unsure whether the highly trained vast armies of Rome can outdo the magic he believes the Britons have on their side. He may ask the time travellers if they believe in magic and if they think he will be okay.

Roman weaponry

A short sword Marcus laughs at the swords of the Britons, which are long and unwieldy. He has been trained to use the short sword, which enables precision. (He hasn't actually killed before and may be a bit anxious about the thought of it. A short sword means being very close to the victim.)

Two javelins The soldiers may only throw their javelins on command. The enemy is showered twice by volleys of javelins. The Britons throw spears that could be hurled back at them by their enemy. The Romans' superior design ensured no Romans could be killed by their own weapons: the head of the javelin broke off on impact. Marcus will be proud of this and can demonstrate how a javelin is thrown.

Rectangular curved shield The shields are designed so that the soldiers can stand close to one another holding their shields tilted in front of them, protecting themselves to the front and above. The shields touch edges so that the arrows and spears of the Britons hit the shields and cannot harm the soldiers. Marcus may 'show' the large projection in the centre of his shield. It is used to batter enemy soldiers. It looks pretty lethal.

Helmet The Roman helmet makes Marcus feel better. It is so large that the enemy will think that he is bigger than he really is. They will then be frightened of him. He mimes putting the helmet on, asking the time travellers not to be afraid! He strokes the large imagined plume explaining that it gives height. He strokes his hand down his cheeks to show them where the pieces of metal come down to protect his face. There is also curved metal at the back of the neck.

Armour The Roman design consists of narrow strips of metal running horizontally across the body. The metal strips are joined at the top and bottom by tiny metal rings. The soldiers can therefore move about very easily and comfortably, and their armour is not as heavy as solid plate armour.

Britons in battle

Marcus scorns the untrained methods of the Britons. (His only fear is of magic.) The wealthier Britons have two horse chariots on which they ride across the front of the Romans to throw their spears. Britons also use long swords, and bows and arrows, and slings and stones. Some have armour that restricts their movements and must have been heavy to wear. Shields were a variety of shapes and sizes, often with patterns or pictures.

A Roman view of Britons

Marcus knows that some Britons have been 'sensible' and appreciative of what the Romans have done for Britain – the towns and roads. He believes that they are lucky to be learning Latin and Roman 'civilised' ways. It is a mystery to him why other Britons have been so rebellious and unappreciative. Marcus has heard of a crazy woman called Boudica, whose father was a friend to the Romans. She is now stirring up trouble in East Anglia and Marcus will have to march over there when they have sorted out the Druids on Anglesey.

The Druids seem a strange lot to Marcus. They seem to know a lot about nature, the seasons and crops. He is disgusted because he has heard that there is a wood that is sacred to the Druids on Anglesey. There they make human sacrifices to their gods. (The Romans had given up human sacrifices at this stage.) The Druids have consistently resisted the Romans and have continually been defeated. They have fled to or gathered in Anglesey. Marcus may have heard rumours that there is good corn or even gold under the ground on Anglesey, but understands that the invasion is to put a stop to these people who have caused the Romans such trouble, once and for all.

Chapter 11

The Lady of Shalott
A classic text (poem)

The children are given various tasks that provide rich, varied and active ways of studying Tennyson's poem. They create images to accompany lines of the poem, create formal readings of sections, consider genre and its impact for different presentations of the story line, as well as engage in improvised discussion about the Lady of Shalott's death.

Age group	9–11 years
Curriculum area focus	**English** Looking at a classic poem. Increasing ability to read, with fluency and accuracy, challenging and lengthy texts. Reflecting on the meaning of texts, analysing and discussing them with others. Using inference and deduction. Considering poetic forms and their effects.
Speaking and listening	Speaking audibly and clearly. Speaking with confidence. Choosing material relevant to the topic. Speaking effectively as a member of a group.
PSHE and Citizenship	Resolving differences by looking at alternatives. Making decisions and explaining choices in small group work.
Resources	Tennyson's 'The Lady of Shalott' is provided (see Figure 11.1).

Time	This extended exploration could be carried out over a period of days or weeks. The total time is approximately four hours and fifteen minutes.

1. These activities are mostly carried out in small groups. The children can change or remain in the same groups.
2. Not all the activities are essential. There is not such a strong sequential significance in this drama as in many of the others in this book.

1. What's a romantic heroine? (10 minutes)

[Class discussion]
Invite discussion about what a romantic heroine would be like. It may be helpful to take the two words separately first. Some suggestions of women thought to be romantic heroines could be discussed, such as Sleeping Beauty, Beauty in *Beauty and the Beast*, Shakespeare's Juliet.

2. Physical image of a romantic heroine (10 minutes)

[Small group sculpting]
In small groups children position a volunteer into an image that they think suitable for a romantic heroine. They can experiment with, for example, where the eyes should look, the tilt of the head, position of feet and hands. It doesn't matter at this stage if it is funny or exaggerated.

3. Reorganising the images and poem extracts (30 minutes)

[Small group discussion and re-forming of sculptured image]
Explain to the children that in the next activity they will be asked to re-form their sculptures and listen to some extracts of a poem about a romantic heroine. After each extract the groups discuss how they will add to and/or amend their image to take into account the new information. Each extract could be displayed in written form after it has been read out, to enable the children to re-read to check the details.

Extract 1
> *Four grey walls, and four grey towers,*
> *Overlook a space of flowers,*

Here for example, groups may wish to represent the wall around the woman, the towers and/or the flowers. They can use chairs if they like.

Extract 2
> *There she weaves by night and day*
> *A magic web with colours gay.*

Groups now consider how this will change their sculpture, and reform it.

Extract 3
> *And moving through a mirror clear*
> *That hangs before her all the year,*
> *Shadows of the world appear.*

Again, each group considers how this may affect their image and make any changes they choose. Children may need help here to understand the reference to the reflections in the mirror.

Extract 4
> *Out flew the web and floated wide;*
> *The mirror cracked from side to side;*
> *'The curse has come upon me,' cried*
> *The Lady of Shalott.*

A final readjustment of the image is made in each group.

4. Making sense of the fragments (10 minutes)

[Whole class discussion]
Read all the extracts with a discussion of interesting words and phrases that may need clarification, such as 'a magic web with colours gay'. Ask the children what sense they have made of the lines:

Who have we met in the poem?

What do you think is happening?

What do you think the setting might be like?

What atmosphere is created?

Which words or phrases helped to create the atmosphere?

How did the sculptures help you to understand the lines of the poem?

Tell the children that the poem is 'The Lady of Shalott' by Alfred, Lord Tennyson. You may choose to give a little information about the poet, but it is not necessary for this lesson plan.

5. Words in action (20 minutes)

[Group presentation]

Groups are given a copy of the lines read above. Their task is to repeat the four sculptures they have created to depict the extracts, but this time they select a few words from each extract to accompany each of the sculptures. They must prepare how the words are said and should consider (i) volume, (ii) speed, and (iii) pauses.

They can decide whether they whisper, repeat, chant or even sing the words that are selected. They should then practise moving from one image to the next with the lines.

Variations of this activity include:

- Each group is given only one of the extracts to work on with the one appropriate sculpture.
- Some groups are given particular words or phrases to use.
- The groups present their work. After each performance discussion should focus on the effect of the chosen words and their delivery in relation to the sculpture.

Which words do you remember the group using?

How were they spoken?

Which bits were louder than others?

What was the effect of the changing volume?

What mood did they create?

Are there any changes that could be made to emphasise the atmosphere?

How did the sound-scape relate to the sculpture?

What did the sculpture tell us?

6. Prediction (10 minutes)

[Small group predictions]

Each group discusses:
- what happened to The Lady of Shalott in the past;
- how the narrative could end.

Each group selects someone to report their prediction to the class.

7. How the poem ends (20 minutes)

[Small group mime and teacher reading]

Read the final extract and then give the children a copy. In their groups, the children plan how they can provide actions to accompany the teacher's reading of the verse. A few of them could be the knights crossing themselves as they look down at the boat.

They should discuss how they could make Lancelot look distinct from the others.

> *Who is this? and what is here?*
> *And in the lighted palace near*
> *Died the sound of royal cheer;*
> *And they crossed themselves for fear,*
> *   All the knights at Camelot:*
> *But Lancelot mused a little space;*
> *He said, 'She has a lovely face;*
> *God in His mercy lend her grace,*
> *   The Lady of Shalott.'*

Teacher reads through the verse aloud and all groups perform at the same time. Some may choose to show the others their work afterwards.

8. The story is told (30 minutes)

[Teacher in role]
The purpose of this activity is to give the children the plot of the poem and access to some of Tennyson's language. A narrative is provided which gives the outline of the story and includes various quotations. The children are asked to imagine that they live in or around Camelot. There are different ways that this activity can be run.

(a) The diary
In this approach, the teacher takes on the role of an old woman from Camelot who reads to the class from her diary. She tells the class that she has been looking at the diary entry she wrote a year ago to the day. It makes her think about what a strange world it is. The diary entry recalls what took place in Camelot a year ago and tells of the rumours surrounding a very strange incident.

At times throughout the reading the teacher in role as the old lady pauses to ask if the children have any questions, whether they believe her, if they have heard similar rumours about the story. This breaks up the narrative and ensures an understanding of what has been read. Some suggestions for questions to ask the children are provided in the body of the narrative which follows.

(b) Sharing a memory
In this alternative approach the teacher needs to be familiar with the narrative before she begins so that she can tell it as a story rather than read it as an imaginary diary. She is an old lady who wants to share her memories of a strange incident with the children. She tells them what she remembers. It is important for the teacher to include some of the quotations taken from the poem. Questions can be asked in the same way to keep the interest of the children.

'It was all so strange. No one even knew for sure that anyone lived in the <u>four grey walls, and four grey towers</u> on the little island. My husband was a reaper then, and he said they used to hear someone singing when they were out <u>reaping early In among the bearded barley</u> in the morning. They used to have a joke that some half believed and others wanted to believe that there was a 'Fairy Lady of Shalott' up in the casement window, high up in one of the towers. It's funny to think that so many people passed that way <u>Down to towered Camelot,</u> and yet nobody ever saw her.'

You must have passed by there sometimes. Did you ever look up at the casement window?

Were any of you reapers? Did you hear the singing from the tower?

Do you think people called her a fairy lady as a joke or did they really think there was something magical or mysterious?

'Some time after she was found dead in the boat, people from Camelot went up to her room. They couldn't believe what they found in the room. There was a loom, <u>A magic web with colours gay,</u> and many woven pictures of scenes that she must have seen from the window. But remember that she was never, ever seen looking out of the window. I have <u>heard a whisper say, A curse is on her if she stay To look down to Camelot.</u> So until this day, she never did look out to Camelot. They soon found out how she was able to see who passed. There was a huge mirror. But here is the oddest thing. The mirror was cracked. Not just cracked, but <u>cracked from side to side.</u> Those who went to the room said there was a very mournful feeling. They felt a strange power in there. It was almost as though there was some magic in the room.'

Did any of you go into the tower?

How would you describe the atmosphere?

Would it really have been possible for her to see what went on outside through the mirror?

Could it have been a practical joke? After all there are a lot of youngsters with a strange sense of humour these days!

'Now, you may have heard about this curse. Of course, no one knows why there should have been a curse on such a beautiful young lady, nor what exactly the curse could have been. One thing is certain. The curse came upon her the day that Lancelot passed by. You may have heard about him. He was one of King Arthur's Knights of the Round Table. Well, many folk say that she saw the reflection of him riding past in the mirror. <u>The bridle-bells rang merrily As he rode down to Camelot. The helmet and the helmet-feather Burned like one burning flame together.</u> She couldn't help herself. She turned to look directly through the window. It was this that seems to have brought about her doom. There are those who were on the river that day who swear they heard the crack that tore the mirror apart and the crash as it fell in splinters to the ground.'

Did any of you see Sir Lancelot?

Was he so good looking to turn a poor girl's head?

Did any of you hear the crash of the mirror?

'They saw her leave the towers, looking so calm, as though she was in a trance. She was dressed in a snowy white robe. <u>Down she came and found a boat Beneath a willow left afloat</u>. That was an odd coincidence. It was as though the boat was meant to be there for her. <u>Round about the prow she wrote 'The Lady of Shallot'</u>. In the boat <u>she floated down to Camelot</u>. Can you imagine what a sight it was! You may wonder why nobody approached her. She had an air of mystery about her. Poor girl. <u>They heard her singing her last song</u>. Can you believe that she sang as she lay in that boat? Sang, that is, until <u>her blood was frozen slowly</u>.

As people gathered around the boat they were afraid and crossed themselves to keep any bad spirits away. That's how mysterious the whole thing was. As for Sir Lancelot, well, all he had to say was, '<u>She has a lovely face; God in His mercy lend her grace, The Lady of Shalott</u>.' I don't know what to make of any of it.'

Do you think she died of cold or was it of love, or of loneliness, or was it the curse?

What do you make of all this?

Some discussion about what they have heard will follow led by the teacher out of role:

Do you believe the old woman's story?

Do you think that the old woman believed the story herself?

How do you think that she got her information?

With whom do you think she sympathised?

What was her attitude to The Lady and Sir Lancelot?

(c) A further option
Teacher can tell the class that the story includes many extracts from the poem. She reads the narrative again (or for the first time) and the children should clap their hands when they think they have heard phrases that they guess may have come from the poem. Teacher may wish to indicate with a gesture when the quotations appear, letting the children know when they are right.

Teachers may choose to read the whole poem to the children now that they know the plot and have heard the style of the language (see Figure 11.1 p. 108–10).

9. Group formal readings (30 minutes)

[Group planning for readings]
Rearrange the class into five groups. Part IV of the poem contains six

verses. Each group is given one verse excluding the last verse which they already know. Each group must discuss and prepare a formal reading of their verse. They will stand in a line to read it. They should consider some or all of the following questions:

1. Which lines should be louder/softer than others?
2. Which words or phrases need to be stressed?
3. When should there be many voices and when just a single voice?
4. Would any gestures help convey meaning through the reading?
5. Where should there be moments of silence, pauses between words or lines?
6. Are there any examples of figurative language?
7. What is the effect of the repetition?
8. Is there any significance in the sentence structure?

Questions can be allocated differently for each group's ability.

- Lower ability groups: Questions 1–3. Focus on the difference that volume will make to a reading of the verse. Children can be asked to underline, highlight and annotate the verse with coloured pens to indicate how words are to be read.
- Middle ability groups: Questions 1–5. Focus on the difference between hearing a poem read aloud and reading it silently. Children answer the questions by underlining, highlighting and annotating the verse with coloured pens. They discuss the effect such a reading might have on listeners.
- High ability groups: Questions 1–9. Focus on the figurative language used by Tennyson. They look for metaphors, similes and adjectives, for example. Ask them to underline, highlight and annotate the verse with coloured pens to indicate how it will be read aloud.

The groups, in turn, perform their verse in the order of the poem. The audiences can be invited to talk about the effect of each group's reading, the atmospheres they created, and the clarity of delivery. Groups may then wish to explain their choices and intentions.

10. Playing with genre (45 minutes)

[Small group story telling with images]
Discuss genres such as horror, romance, mock horror, science fiction, sitcom, and detective. The following questions may all be discussed with the class as a whole, or a list of features of one genre, such as horror, could be made with the class, to serve as an example. Groups could discuss and produce lists of features of the other genres in the list.

What do we expect in horror stories?

And what about mock horror (for example, the film 'Dracula, Dead and Loving It')?

What kind of characters do we find in detective stories/films/television programmes?

What do we expect of romances?

What do we expect of science fiction stories?

What sorts of things do we expect to find in comedy?

Groups of four or five are allocated a particular genre. They must deliver the following verse in the given genre. A romance will need an exaggerated dreamy expression, a horror requries looks of shock and surprise, detectives may be like well-known media figures, while the comic rendering may include slapstick humour. The groups read the lines accompanied by action. Some groups may wish to have one reader. Others may decide to share out the lines as they engage in the action.

> *She left the web, she left the loom,*
> *She made three paces through the room,*
> *She saw the water-lily bloom,*
> *She saw the helmet and the plume,*
> > *She looked down to Camelot.*
> *Out flew the web and floated wide;*
> *The mirror cracked from side to side;*
> *'The curse is come upon me,' cried*
> > *The Lady Of Shalott.*

11. Narrative gap: the curse (30 minutes)

[Small group playmaking]
Groups of about five children discuss how and why they think the curse may have been put on the Lady of Shalott in the first place. They should remember the key elements of walls, magic web, and mirror. They need to keep the feel of the poem's landscape and era. Once they have agreed upon their story of the curse they can do one of the following tasks:

- present their story with accompanying images sculpted as in activity 1;
- tell their story as a choral speaking presentation as in activity 9;
- enact the story.

Additional possibilities

1. Individual written activity
    Write individual stories of the origins of the curse.
2. Individual drawing and extract selection activity
    Draw a series of pictures to depict the narrative of the poem. Select one appropriate line from the poem to write underneath each picture as a caption.
3. Oral pair activity
    In pairs prepare a conversation that could have occurred between two gossips living near the four grey towers, after they have heard about the woman's death.
4. Individual written activity
    After activity 8 'The story is told', children can be given the list of

quotations used in the narrative. They imagine that they are people who were also living in Camelot last year. Children individually write diary entries telling the events from the point of view of someone else – whoever the children wish to be! They can be cynical, frightened, spiritual or melodramatic, but they must include all (or some) of the quotations provided in the list.

5. ICT opportunity

    Images of Pre-Raphaelite paintings can be downloaded from the Internet. There are many sites with the paintings of William John Waterhouse and William Holman Hunt. Examples include: www.nouveaunet.com and www.pre-raphaelites.com

    Children can select particular paintings of The Lady of Shalott and decide which lines of the poem could be presented with each painting.

    Another exciting ICT opportunity is to photograph some of the sculpture made in the drama activities with a digital camera. Once on screen children can add sounds that would be appropriate with the images. These could include lines from the poem, perhaps sung or whispered. The images from the sculptures can also be manipulated on screen to heighten the effects.

Part I

ON either side the river lie
Long fields of barley and of rye,
That clothe the wold and meet the sky;
And through the field the road runs by
    To many-towered Camelot;
And up and down the people go,
Gazing where the lilies blow
Round an island there below,
    The island of Shalott.

Willows whiten, aspens quiver,
Little breezes dusk and shiver
Through the wave that runs for ever
By the island in the river
    Flowing down to Camelot.
Four grey walls, and four grey towers,
Overlook a space of flowers,
And the silent isle embowers
    The Lady of Shalott.

By the margin, willow-veiled,
Slide the heavy barges trailed
By slow horses; and unhailed
The shallop flitteth silken-sailed
    Skimming down to Camelot.
But who hath seen her wave her hand?
Or at the casement seen her stand?
Or is she known in all the land,
    The Lady of Shalott?

Only reapers reaping early
In among the bearded barley,
Hear a song that echoes cheerly
From the river winding clearly,
    Down to towered Camelot:
And by the moon the reaper weary,
Piling sheaves in uplands airy,
Listening, whispers ''Tis the fairy
    Lady of Shalott.'

Part II

There she weaves by night and day
A magic web with colours gay.
She has heard a whisper say,
A curse is on her if she stay
    To look down to Camelot.
She knows not what the curse may be,
And so she weaveth steadily,
And little other care hath she,
    The Lady of Shalott.

And moving through a mirror clear
That hangs before her all the year,
Shadows of the world appear.
There she sees the highway near
    Winding down to Camelot:
There the river eddy whirls,
And there the surly village-churls,
And the red cloaks of market girls,
    Pass onward from Shalott.

Sometimes a troop of damsels glad,
An abbot on an ambling pad,
Sometimes a curly shepherd-lad,
Or long-haired page in crimson clad,
   Goes by to towered Camelot;
And sometimes through the mirror blue
The knights come riding two and two:
She hath no loyal knight and true,
   The Lady of Shalott.

But in her web she still delights
To weave the mirror's magic sights,
For often through the silent nights
A funeral, with plumes and lights,
   And music, went to Camelot.
Or when the moon was overhead,
Came two young lovers lately wed;
'I am half sick of shadows,' said
   The Lady of Shalott.

      Part III
A bow-shot from her bower-eaves,
He rode between the barley-sheaves,
The sun came dazzling through the leaves,
And flamed upon the brazen greaves
   Of bold Sir Lancelot.
A red-cross knight for ever kneeled
To a lady in his shield,
That sparkled on the yellow field,
   Beside remote Shalott.

The gemmy bridle glittered free,
Like to some branch of stars we see
Hung in the golden Galaxy.
The bridle-bells rang merrily
   As he rode down to Camelot:
And from his blazoned baldric slung
A mighty silver bugle hung,
And as he rode his armour rung,
   Beside remote Shalott.

All in the blue unclouded weather
Thick-jewelled shone the saddle-leather,
The helmet and the helmet-feather
Burned like one burning flame together,
   As he rode down to Camelot.
As often through the purple night,
Below the starry clusters bright,
Some bearded meteor, trailing light,
   Moves over still Shalott.

His broad clear brow in sunlight glowed;
On burnished hooves his war-horse
   trode;

From underneath his helmet flowed
His coal-black curls as on he rode,
   As he rode down to Camelot.
From the bank and from the river
He flashed into the crystal mirror,
'Tirra lirra,' by the river
   Sang Sir Lancelot.

She left the web, she left the loom,
She made three paces through the room,
She saw the water-lily bloom,
She saw the helmet and the plume,
   She looked down to Camelot.
Out flew the web and floated wide;
The mirror cracked from side to side;
'The curse is come upon me,' cried
   The Lady of Shalott.

      Part IV
In the stormy east-wind straining,
The pale yellow woods were waning,
The broad stream in his banks
   complaining,
Heavily the low sky raining
   Over towered Camelot;
Down she came and found a boat
Beneath a willow left afloat,
And round the prow she wrote
   'The Lady of Shalott'.

And down the river's dim expanse—
Like some bold seër in a trance,
Seeing all his own mischance—
With a glassy countenance
   Did she look to Camelot.
And at the closing of the day
She loosed the chain and down she lay;
The broad stream bore her far away,
   The Lady of Shalott.

Lying, robed in snowy white—
That loosely flew to left and right—
The leaves upon her falling light—
Through the noises of the night
   She floated down to Camelot:
And as the boat-head wound along
The willowy hills and fields among,
They heard her singing her last song,
   The Lady of Shalott.

Heard a carol, mournful, holy,
Chanted loudly, chanted lowly,
Till her blood was frozen slowly,
And her eyes were darkened wholly,

Turned to towered Camelot;
For ere she reached upon the tide
The first house by the water-side,
Singing in her song she died,
　　The Lady of Shalott.

Under tower and balcony,
By garden-wall and gallery,
A gleaming shape she floated by,
Dead-pale between the houses high,
　　Silent into Camelot.
Out upon the wharfs they came,
Knight and burgher, lord and dame,

And round the prow they read her name,
　　'The Lady of Shalott'.

Who is this? and what is here?
And in the lighted palace near
Died the sound of royal cheer;
And they crossed themselves for fear,
　　All the knights at Camelot:
But Lancelot mused a little space;
He said, 'She has a lovely face;
God in His mercy lend her grace,
　　The Lady of Shalott.'

ALFRED, LORD TENNYSON

Figure 11.1 The Lady of Shalott

Chapter 12

The Reds and the Greens
Understanding prejudice

The children are in role as members of the Red community, hardworking and living in a happy and peaceful land. That is, until their ruler dies and is replaced by a Green leader who decrees that things will have to change. The Reds will not be allowed to live and behave as before but will follow new Green laws that go against their traditional practices. There is disruption in the community unsettling their peaceful existence. The Reds have been put in a very difficult position. How will they respond?

Age group	7–11 years
Curriculum area focus	**Citizenship**
Speaking and listening	Creating, adapting and sustaining different roles, individually and in groups. Asking relevant questions. Responding appropriately. Dealing politely with opposing views.
PSHE and Citizenship	Why and how laws are made and enforced. Recognising the consequences of anti-social and aggressive behaviours, such as bullying and racism, on individuals and communities. Reflecting on moral, social and cultural issues, using imagination to understand other people's experiences. Democracy.
Resources	Red stickers. Green stickers. Red cloak, scarf, jumper or other item.

Green cloak, scarf, jumper or other item.
A large book with a red cover.
A scroll with the decree written on it (see Figure 12.1).

Time   The whole session takes about one and a half hours.

1. This drama raises a number of difficult issues to do with prejudice, imposing ideas on others, loyalty and freedom to follow your own beliefs. Issues concerned with repression, ethnic cleansing, religious, racial and political freedom can be raised through this session depending on your focus.
2. Originally, this drama was written as a way into the religious issues raised during the Tudor and Stuart period in British history which resulted in the Gunpowder Plot. It is useful to bear this in mind though as the struggle between the Reds and the Greens closely echoes that between the Catholics and the Protestants. However, it has far wider possible connections.
3. The colours red and green have been chosen as clearly different and identifiable colours but any two contrasting colours, shapes or symbols can be chosen if these two are not appropriate for your situation. The Suns and the Moons, the Circles and the Triangles, the Purples and the Yellows are all perfectly acceptable. Suitable stickers and cloaks (or other token items of costume) will need to be found.

Notes

1. Setting the scene – the people of the Red land (5 minutes)

Drama activities

[Ritual and teacher in role]
The children stand in a circle and, one at a time, are solemnly and formally given red stickers to wear. Tell them that in the drama these are known as emblems and are worn with great pride.

Tell the children that they are all people of the Red land waiting on the quiet hillside outside their village for an important event to occur. Tell them that you will walk away and then return to the circle in role as someone that they all know, and you will speak to them. They must listen carefully to pick up clues and information to find out more about the drama and who they are in it.

Walk away from the circle, put on the red cloak and slowly return, smiling calmly, looking positive, and authoritative. Address the people:

My friends, people of the Red land. We gather here today on this quiet hillside as we do every year to think about our precious Red land and the Queen who rules so fairly and justly over us all. We think of what it means to be a Red and how important our Red laws have become, helping to keep our community safe and happy for so long. These Red laws that we all live by were written down in the time of Aelfric the Red, our first leader, and agreed on by all of the people. The law decrees that we should wear our Red emblems with pride, eat the food of the Reds, wear the clothes of the Reds and lead our lives in the ways agreed.

2. What have we learned? (5 minutes)

[Discussion]
Take off the cloak and sit down in a circle. Ask the group about what has just happened.

Who are the people standing on the hillside?

Why are the people wearing red emblems?

Who was the person in the red cloak?

What event is taking place?

Is there any sense of a time period for the drama?

What gives this impression?

What could the speaker have meant about the Red laws? What could they be?

Why could it be that these laws are so important to the Reds?

What sort of community is this?

Issues concerning why and how rules and laws are made can be discussed here.

3. The Red laws (20 minutes)

[Still pictures with captions]
Tell the class that you are going to discover more about the Red land and its people, in particular their laws. Discuss possibilities such as:

- eating Red food;
- wearing Red clothes;
- rituals to remember the great Aelfric the Red;
- a Red celebration;
- a Red greeting.

Divide the class into small groups of four or five. Ask each group to decide on one aspect of the Red law and create a still picture to show the other groups. You could tell the children that these pictures are taken from a book about the Red land and its people and that it illustrates aspects of their culture. If you have a large red book use this as a prop. Ask each group to think of the caption that would go underneath their picture and write it on a large piece of paper.

Each group shows their picture and the rest of the class tries to decide upon what is being shown. The captions are then read. Teacher introduces each new picture solemnly and thanks each group for showing an important aspect of the Red law.

After all of the pictures have been viewed reiterate the importance of the laws and how important the book of Red Law is to the people.

4. A threat to the peace of the Red land (10 minutes)

[Teacher in role and meeting]
Ask the group to reform the circle and tell them that in the next part of the drama you will be someone that they haven't met before. Leave the circle and put on the Green cloak. Return to the circle carrying the scroll. Try to create a different atmosphere this time. Walk slowly and look around at the Reds as though they were beneath you. Be powerful and aloof, perhaps threatening, but not over the top! Slowly unroll the scroll and read.

The Queen of this land is dead. The new King decrees that from this day no one is to wear the clothes of the Reds, eat the food of the Reds or follow any of the Red laws as written by Aelfric the Red, the first leader of the Red people. The people of the Red land must never again wear their Red emblems or gather together on the quiet hillside as they have done in the past each year. They will now abide by the laws of the Green King and wear Green emblems or risk severe punishment. The Reds have been warned!

King James

©Ackroyd, J. and Boulton, J. (2001) *Drama Lessons for Five to Eleven-Year-Olds*. London: David Fulton Publishers. www.fultonpublishers.co.uk

Figure 12.1 The Green message

Tell the Reds that you are able to answer a few questions before you leave but as you are only the messenger you have no real answers. Any difficult questions that are asked can be answered with a cutting phrase such as:

You have been told what will happen if you do not obey.

There is no option.

You have no choice.

The King has decreed so that is the end to it.

5. How do we feel about this? (10 minutes)

[Thought tunnel]
Ask the group to stand in two parallel lines facing each other with enough space for you to walk down the 'path' that has been created. Explain that you are going to walk down this path as though you were the Green messenger leaving the village. Ask them to speak their thoughts about the situation such as:

This is terrible.

They can't do this.

I'm not going to follow any Green laws.

I'll always be a Red.

As the Green messenger passes along the path he puts a Green sticker or emblem onto each Red and announces:

You will follow the laws of the Green King and wear the Green emblem.

6. Reflection (5 minutes)

[Discussion]
Talk about what has happened so far.

How would the Reds be feeling?

What could they really do about the situation?

What would it feel like to be told you couldn't be yourself any more?

We have found that the children usually say they would fight against the Greens, and the futility of this approach should be discussed. The King is Green and the power is therefore in Green hands.

7. The Reds talk in secret (10 minutes)

[Overheard conversations]
Ask the children to sit in small groups and discuss the feelings of the Reds in role. Ask them to think what the Reds would try to do about the situation. Tell them that you will walk around the village in role as the Green messenger so they must be careful about what they say when you are near. Give all of the groups a few minutes to have a practise at their improvised conversations. Ask each group in turn to talk while the rest listen. As you walk up to the group the subject of the conversation should change quickly to avoid you hearing any Red talk.

8. Spreading rumours around the Red village (10 minutes)

[Chinese whispers game]
Ask the groups to repeat their conversations and this time you will change your cloak and once again be a Red. Go from group to group joining in the conversations and stirring up dissatisfaction.

I'm not going to sit back and take orders from the Green King. Meet me tonight on the quiet hillside to discuss a plan.

9. Challenging the Green King (10 minutes)

[Teacher in role and meeting]

That night under the cover of darkness every single member of the Red people gathered together to discuss what they could do.

Teacher in role as the Red subversive welcomes the Reds and collects them all together, encouraging quietness and secrecy by whispering, looking around nervously, and possibly crouching down.

Develop your subversive role, stirring up anti-Green feeling. Encourage them to wear their Red emblems and throw away the Green ones.

Remember Aelfric and the Red laws. What would he say to see you all forgetting so quickly?

We have found that some children are quick to join the subversive while others are more wary, being mindful of the warning that the Green messenger made and wanting a quiet life. This debate can go on for as long as it is productive and exploring new ideas or possibilities.

10. The Reds are caught out (5 minutes)

[Teacher in role]
Quickly, ask the children to re-form the circle as in activity 1. Change your cloak to Green and rapidly re-enter the circle. Look searchingly around the circle and pick out those who are wearing the Red emblems. Make them stand at one side of the room.

Announce to those who are wearing Red emblems:

You were warned. Now you will be punished!

11. What will the future hold? (10 minutes)

[Discussion; circle of thoughts]
Talk about what has happened.

115

What do the children think will happen to the Red dissidents?

What will the rest feel?

How will life change for the Reds?

Tell the children that to finish off the drama they are going to speak the thoughts and feelings of the Red people. Place a chair in the middle of the room with the Red book on it. Ask the children to stand either in a circle around the chair or randomly around the room. If you choose to ask them to stand randomly, ask them to think about how near to the book they want to stand. This will be determined by how loyal they feel towards Aelfric or how much they feel they have betrayed the Red laws. Some may also choose to stand with their backs to the book or some may want to kneel down.

When the positions have been chosen, you will go around and touch each child on the shoulder. The children will speak aloud the thoughts of their roles.

I know I have betrayed Aelfric's laws.

I feel dreadful.

What could we have done? I'll always wear a Red emblem under my cloak.

12. Reflection on the drama (10 minutes)

[Discussion]
It is important to spend some time after the drama has finished to discuss the issues raised and relate this story to a historical or topical context.

Additional possibilities

1. Individual writing activity
   Children write a legend about Aelfric the Red which tells of his strength and wisdom.
2. Individual, group or whole class writing
   The Red laws and the Green laws or customs can be written in a list.
3. Small group drama activity
   Imagine that an old Green book is discovered. It contains pictures and captions just like the Red book in activity 3. In groups, children make the Green pictures as they did for the Red book.
4. Writing activity
   Compose a letter from the Red people to the Green King to plead their case.
5. Pair writing activity
   Children write out a new decree on a scroll. Imagine now that the Green King dies and the next Queen is a Red. Write the new declaration that might be issued with this ascension. Consider the previous declaration (see Figure 12.1) and the reaction to it. Is this new decree to restrict the rights of the Greens, or is it respecting the differences in the realm?

Chapter 13

Where's the blame?

A drama script; Bullying

Working from the first scene of Calcutt's *The Terrible Fate of Humpty Dumpty* (Published by Nelson Thornes Ltd, Cheltenham, extract given in Figure 13.1), in which a bullied schoolboy is accidentally executed on a pylon, the children go back in time to look at what led to this tragedy. They are invited to explore both the minds of the 'gang' and the bullied Terry, and, most significantly, the responsibility of those who were silent observers.

Age group	10–11 years
Curriculum area focus	**English** Play text
Speaking and listening	Recognising language variation according to context and purpose: formal interviews, private emotional language, language of power, manipulative language, coercive language. Identifying features of language used for a specific purpose. Improvisation and working in role. Reading aloud.
PSHE and Citizenship	Bullying, social responsibility, empathy. Realising the consequences of anti-social and aggressive behaviours.
Resources	David Calcutt's *The Terrible Fate of Humpty Dumpty*, scenes one and two (see Figure 13.1). A cleared space in the classroom or activity room/hall.
Time	This work will take a minimum of three and a half hours.

Notes

1. Don't let the horrific notion of an electrocuted child put you off this drama. Children deal with it very well and the shock of the dramatic event takes them into a serious approach to the work. We recommend the play for a class reader:
   The Terrible Fate of Humpty Dumpty, by David Calcutt is published in the Dramascripts series by Nelson Thornes (1998). It can be purchased in hard cover or paper back.
2. It is important to see these activities through to the end where a positive resolution can be explored.
3. Children work as a whole group in moving the text into performance. They later work in small groups.
4. Reading from the text is followed by exploration of performance ideas, but there is also improvisation and small group devised scenes.

Drama activities

1. Reading the text (10 minutes)

[Class play reading]
Each child is given a copy of scene one and parts are allocated. The remaining children read for the gang. The stage directions are read with feeling by the teacher to create the haunting atmosphere.

2. Intimidation with no words (15 minutes)

[Discussion and practical exploration]
In this activity words are not relevant. Consideration is given to how gang members may have made Terry feel intimidated without the use of words or physical contact. Teacher or a pupil stands in the centre of the space and invites volunteers one at a time to stand up and try out an intimidating role. They may stand and stare, they may circle, they may smile in a mocking manner. After each individual's attempt there is discussion about the effect and why it was or wasn't successful. They can explore the effect of distance between the two characters, the effect of height, what can be achieved with fast and slow movements and so on.

3. Intimidation scene before the dialogue (20 minutes)

[Whole group devising]
Discuss what might have led up to this moment.

Who had been at the wasteland first?

At what point was Terry aware of the presence of the gang?

How did they make their presence felt?

Had Terry tried to get away, tried to join in, tried to look relaxed, or shown his fear?

Agree some details and then create the scene of Terry and the gang meeting on the wasteland before any words are spoken. This depicts what took place immediately prior to the first scene of the play. No words are spoken in this scene and no physical contact is made. Pupils should draw on their earlier experimentations in activity 2. The challenge is to create a genuinely intimidating atmosphere, involving everyone, that makes what happens next believable.

They can circle, look threatening, circle and stare to lead to the moment where the dialogue begins.

4. 'See my Frisbee, Humpty?' (30 minutes)

[Whole group performance of written text]
The devised intimidation scene is then followed by the enactment of scene one from the script. First agree on what represents the pylon. It could be a chair or a table. Experiment to find ways to enable Terry to climb the pylon slowly enough to build tension, looking up and down, wondering if he will make it. The class agree on how they will show the moment that he dies – for instance, he flops suddenly from the waist.

In preparing to perform the scene, the 'gang' are encouraged to contribute 'yeahs' to continue the threatening atmosphere. Pauses between bits of dialogue need to be considered, so that it is not just one line after another. Pete may look around the space before throwing the frisbee, so that there is a gap in speech at this point. This would draw attention to the moment when he throws it up into the pylon.

The two scenes can be run together as one.

5. Terry's thoughts contrasting with the gang's bravado (20 minutes)

[Thought tracking]
About six volunteers are positioned on chairs around the edge of the performance space. The scenes will be run again, but this time the action is controlled by those on the chairs. When any one of them claps their hands, the action freezes at once – whatever is taking place. The volunteer who has clapped speaks aloud a thought that Humpty may have at that moment.

Why are they all here now?

Maybe if I do this for them, they will leave me alone.

My hands are slipping on the metal – I won't make it.

After each thought, there is a moment's pause and then the action continues again until the next clap is heard. The volunteers need to clap a few times for it to be most effective in slowing down the action and inviting scrutiny on what took place and the contrast between the individual's thoughts and the spoken words. It doesn't matter how close to each other the claps are.

6. Reading the second scene from the play script (10 minutes)

[Class play reading]
Read the second scene with parts allocated. Again, teacher reads the stage directions.

7. Stubbs considers the implications (10 minutes)

[Active brainstorm of thoughts]

What might Stubbs be thinking on seeing Terry die?

A few suggestions are heard. The next activity is to explore the range and rush of thoughts, feelings and fears that will fill Stubbs's head.

Terry is positioned hanging on the 'pylon'. The gang are spread about the space at the moment Terry has just died. Stubbs is asked to move between the others, turning and twisting to represent his mind moving from one thought to another. He should stop in front of one gang member after another. As he does, the gang member responds by speaking aloud a thought that could be in Stubbs's mind:

Will Sammy grass on us?

I've gone too far this time.

Dumpton wasn't that bad.

Why did he go on climbing?

8. Ritualistic threat to Sammy (10 minutes)

[Statementing]
Sammy has been identified as the weak link. He is seated in the centre of the space. The rest of the children stand around at some distance as gang members. They have gathered together to ensure that Sammy will not say a word to anyone about what happened.

Each one moves forward to Sammy and voices a threat. Stubbs should be the first to move in. Having said his lines, each moves back to keep Sammy looking isolated and giving room for the next one to go in.

You tell and you'll get it.

Don't forget that you were there, too.

You say a word and we'll tell them how you forced Terry up there.

9. Previous incidents of bullying Terry (20 minutes)

[Small group playmaking]
Tell the class that Sammy was left thinking back to what had gone before. He remembers so many incidents where Terry was teased, threatened, bullied by the gang.

What sort of incidents might these be?

Small groups devise scenes that depict earlier incidents. They may take place in the playground after school, in the classroom, and elsewhere. Each scene should freeze at the moment when the bullying behaviour peaks to maximum. These are performed.

Discussion should focus on how convincing the scenes were. Groups discuss any improvements they wish to make. These scenes will be used within the next activity.

10. Sammy's statement (20 minutes)

[Whole class performance]
Now the group scenes are brought together into one drama. Teacher in role is Sammy seven months later when at last he has decided to make a statement. He is sitting on a chair recalling the events from when Terry first joined the school, and he describes incidents, which led up to his death. Sammy recalls each of the incidents in the devised scenes, but instead of describing them, the groups get up and perform them.

The class arrange themselves in a horseshoe either side of him and are told before Sammy begins in which order the groups will perform. Teacher in role as Sammy provides the narrative which links the scenes and ends with reference to the wasteland. Below is a brief example of how it should be played.

It seems like yesterday that Terry moved into the area. We sat next to each other in geography and got on pretty well. He was shy, but fun…I knew things were going to be hopeless for him on that first lunchtime. Stubbs came up and stood right in front of him in the lunch queue. 'What yer going to do about it?' Terry had no answer and let him go in front. Stubbs laughed and brought all his gang in front, too. I knew that was it. Terry's life would be hell.

The next day, he was in the playground…

Then the scene in the playground is performed.

That's how it was. Then there was the time…

And so on through the scenes.

And then the next time we all saw him was on the waste ground…

Sammy covers his face with his hands, and can say no more.

11. Advice to Terry (20 minutes)

[Advice forum and teacher in role]
Teacher explains that Sammy wishes he had helped Terry. He could have given him some advice about how to survive Stubbs and his gang.

What advice would have been useful to Terry?

The class is invited to offer Terry the advice that Sammy might have given. Teacher will enter as Terry, with shoulders down and eyes to the ground. Teacher needs to respond to the suggestions, which may include:

Hold your head up.

Keep out of their way.

Look Stubbs straight in the eye.

Terry may attempt to act on what they say:

Do you mean stand like this?

What sort of expression should I have when I look at him?

Does this walk look okay?

He may also reply that he can't, or doesn't know if the suggestion would work. The children may need to think very carefully about what will work.

Note that, for the teacher, it is fascinating that when this takes place in the classroom, those who are bullied are often hearing from those who bully them what sort of things may put an end to bullying. It is a public discussion about what happens between the children, but it is neatly concealed as a drama about a pretend boy. It is therefore safe to discuss. We believe that it is best not to relate bullying incidents in the drama to 'real life' incidents in your school. The children may if they wish, but otherwise they will take from it what they need to take for themselves.

12. What they really thought about Stubbs (10 minutes)

[Statementing]
Class stands in a circle. Place a chair in the centre. It should remain empty, representing Stubbs.

No one would ever say what they thought of Stubbs. They wouldn't dare! Stubbs was too powerful. But, what if, for one moment, they dared...what would they say if they dared just once to tell Stubbs what they really thought of him?

Teacher demonstrates what they will all do: walk into the circle, up to the chair, and speak as though the chair is Stubbs, before returning to their place in the circle. For instance:

You think we like you, but we don't.

Do you ever think what it's like on the other side?

13. Who can we blame? (20 minutes)

[Whole group still image and thought tap]
Ask one of the small groups to recreate the frozen moment of bullying from the end of their scene. A playground scene is ideal. The remaining children stand in a circle around the edge of the space. They are asked to imagine that they were children in the playground that day, and are reminded that everyone knew exactly what was going on.

Where were you standing at this moment when Terry was bullied?

Did you watch?

Did you pretend it wasn't happening?

Did you point it out to your friend?

Were you laughing at it?

Were you running away so as not to get involved?

Did you hope not to be seen by the bullies in case it was you next?

Were you glad they were onto Terry so you were safe?

One at a time and in silence, children move into the space and position themselves in an appropriate gesture indicating a response to questions above. No one should move until the previous person has held his position and there has been time to consider his place in the overall context.

Teacher moves through the final creation and taps individuals on the shoulder. In response the child speaks aloud his imagined thoughts at this moment. Perhaps:

Terry is a weakling.

They have no feelings.

If it wasn't him, it would be me.

Finally, teacher announces that all of them witnessed the bullying of Terry Dumpton. Not one of them did anything. What excuse do they have?

Spend time on a discussion of the responsibility of the onlookers in Terry's suffering. What could they have done?

14. Reconstructing the past (20 minutes)

[Re-form images]
The small groups re-form and discuss how their image could be changed from the moment of peak tension. They can consider the advice given to Terry earlier or at any other moment in the drama. Their task is to change the dynamic in some way that means that Terry emerges 'unscathed'. They then act this out from the moment they had frozen.

They show their new scenes and discuss the implications of the 'ways out' for Terry.

Would they work in real life?

Would there be any repercussions later?

Additional possibilities

1. Individually written diaries and reading aloud
    Children write diary entries of different days in the lives of characters from the play. These can be read aloud. It is interesting to play with the way these diaries are read. The same incident, for example the wasteland incident, could be described by two characters differently. Sammy's diary could be read one sentence at a time alternating with Stubbs's diary a sentence at a time. The two personal accounts of the event are thus juxtaposed and their distinctions highlighted.

2. Small group written tasks
    The children imagine the characters' school reports. For example, Sammy: 'English. Sammy seems to lack concentration at the moment. His work is untidy and full of careless mistakes. This is unusual for Sammy and causing me concern.' These can be collated in small groups, each taking different subjects.

3. Individual creative writing
    The children write the story of *The Terrible Fate of Humpty Dumpty* from the point of view of a character in the story. For example, the children decide what Stubbs's version of events would be and write about them as if they were Stubbs.

4. Small group performance
    The children imagine that they work for a video promotions company and have been asked to create a video that can be used in schools to help combat bullying. They can make up anti-bullying rhymes, catch-phrases and songs. They could choose to include discussion or interviews with those connected with the well-known Terry Dumpton case.

The Terrible Fate of Humpty Dumpty by David Calcutt

SCENE 1

(On the waste ground. **Stubbs,** with the **Members of his Gang** – **Jimmy, Pete, Kathy, Kay, Janet** and **Tracey** – are surrounding **Terry Dumpton. Sammy** stands to one side. **The Group** suddenly comes to life as the introductory music fades)

Pete (to Terry)	See my frisbee, Humpty? My best frisbee, this is. I've had this frisbee for ages. I love it. I'd hate to lose it. I'd go mad if I lost this frisbee. Want to see how it works? (**Pete** throws the frisbee into the air, then he says) Oh dear, it's got stuck in the pylon. What am I going to do now?
Stubbs	You'll have to get it back, Pete.
Pete	I know. Only trouble is, I'm scared of heights. Can't stand them. I get a nosebleed just going to the top of the stairs.
Stubbs	You'll have to get somebody to fetch it down for you, then.
Pete	That's right. Who though? (**Stubbs** points to **Terry**)
Stubbs	Him! (There is a pause. Then **Stubbs** says) All right Humpty? Up you go. Get Pete's frisbee back for him. (There is tension, then **Stubbs** continues) Go on. Climb the pylon. Get it back. (**Terry** stares up at the pylon. **Stubbs** goes on) Perhaps you ain't our mate, then. Perhaps you don't like us at all. That means you're the kind of person who'd sneak on us. (He walks towards **Terry**)
Terry	All right. I'll get it.

Sammy	Don't, Terry.
Stubbs	Shurrup, Sammy.
Sammy	It's dangerous.
Kathy	You wanna go up there instead?
	(There is a pause)
Stubbs	Go on.
	(**Terry** starts to climb the pylon. Egged on by **Pete**, the **Members of the Gang** start to chant 'Humpty Dumpty!' over and over again, and then shout comments up at **Terry**. **Sammy** runs forward)
Sammy	Don't, Terry. Come down.
Stubbs	Shurrup, Sammy, unless you wanna go up after him.
	(The noise continues. Lights suddenly flash on and off. Terry hangs dead from the pylon. The **Members of the Gang** stare up in silence)

SCENE 2

(The **Members of the Gang** turn away from the pylon. They are excited and scared)

Jimmy	Stubbs, what we gonna do?
Janet	Did you see him?
Tracey	He was just hanging there.
Pete	Perhaps he's just having us on. Just a joke, you know.
Kathy	Don't be stupid. You saw the flash.
Tracey	It was an accident. That's what it was, wasn't it? It was just an accident.
Kay	Course, yeah. That's what it was, wasn't it? It was just an accident.

Pete	He was just hanging there. Just hanging there. Like a fried egg! A fried egg! Get it?
	(**Pete** laughs)
Jimmy	Shurrup, will you? Stop laughing. I said stop laughing!
	(He pushes **Pete**)
Pete	Gerroff, Jimmy.
Jimmy	Stop laughing, then, will you?
Pete	All right, I've stopped.
Kathy	Will you two stop it?
Pete	It's him, throwing his weight around.
Kathy	Just stop it. You're getting on my nerves.
Kay	And mine.
Jimmy	What we gonna do, Stubbs? Tell us. What we gonna do?
Janet	I want to go home. I don't want to stay here. I'm going home.
Kathy	No you ain't. You're staying here.
Janet	You can't stop me.
Kathy	Want a bet?
Kay	Yeah, want to bet?
Stubbs	Will you all just shurrup? I'm trying to think.
Kay	It's about time.
Stubbs	And you Kathy. Knock it off. We gotta think what to do.
Tracey	It was an accident wasn't it? It wasn't our fault.
Stubbs	That's right. It was an accident. It wasn't nothing to do with us. We wasn't even here.

Jimmy	What do you mean Stubbs? We wasn't here?
Pete	Listen to what he's got to say, thickhead.
Jimmy	Don't call me thickhead.
Kathy	For God's sake, will you two shurrup?
Stubbs	Right. Listen. This is the story. We wasn't here. We was somewhere else. Down the town. Right? We don't know what happened. We don't know anything about it. Anybody asks us, that's what we tell them. We wasn't here.
Kathy	That's your idea, is it?
Stubbs	Yeah. Why? You got a better one?
Pete	What about my frisbee?
Stubbs	Your what?
Pete	My frisbee.
Tracey	Dumpton's dead, and all he can think about is his frisbee.
Pete	It's important. My frisbee's still up there.
Stubbs	Has it got your name on it?
Pete	No . . .
Stubbs	Well, it don't matter then, does it?
Jimmy	Thickhead.
Janet	We ought to phone for an ambulance. We ought to tell somebody.
Pete	Ambulance ain't no good for him now. It's a hearse he needs.
Janet	You're sick, you are.
Tracey	Janet's right. We ought to tell somebody. The police.

Stubbs	We ain't telling nobody!
Janet	We can't just leave him up there.
Stubbs	You wanna drop us all in it? Is that what you want? You know what'll happen if they find out.
Kathy	Stubbs is right. We've all gotta stick together now. Stick to the same story. That's the only thing we can do.
Kay	Yeah. That's right.
Stubbs	Everybody agreed then? Right?
Janet	I suppose so. As long as I can go home. I don't feel very well.
Kathy	You can go home now. Just make sure you don't say anything.
Janet	I won't.
Tracey	I'm coming with you.
	(**Janet** and **Tracey** go)
Pete	I'm going as well. See you tomorrow.
Stubbs	See you, Pete.
	(**Pete** goes)
Kathy	(Pointing to **Sammy**). What about him?
Stubbs	Leave him to me. He won't be no trouble.
Kathy	Just make sure of it.
Stubbs	I will!
Kathy	Come on Kay.
	(**Kathy** and **Kay** go)
Stubbs	You got the story straight, Sammy?
Sammy	What?

Stubbs	Got the story? We weren't here.
Sammy	We killed him.
Stubbs	I'm warning you.
Sammy	We killed him. It was us. We did that.
Stubbs	Jimmy. See to him.
	(**Jimmy** grabs **Sammy**. Then **Stubbs** says)
	Now listen, Sammy. You're in this with the rest of us. So don't you go talking to anybody about it. Right? 'Cos if you do, it ain't just the police you'll have to worry about. You'll have to worry about Jimmy here making such a mess of your face that nobody'll ever recognise you again. They won't even know if you was a human being. Ain't that right Jimmy?
Jimmy	Yeah. That's right.
Stubbs	So just remember, Sammy. Remember whose side you're on.
	(There is a pause. Then **Stubbs** says)
	Come on Jimmy.
	(**Jimmy** looses **Sammy**)
Jimmy	Remember, Sammy.
	(**Stubbs** and **Jimmy** go. Then **Sammy** looks up at **Terry's** body)
Sammy	Terry . . . I'm sorry . . . I tried to help but . . . I'm sorry . . .
	(He faces the **Audience**, and says)
	We killed him!
	(He runs off)

Figure 13.1 *The Terrible Fate of Humpty Dumpty* by David Calcutt. Extract reproduced by kind permission of Nelson Thornes Ltd. © Nelson Thornes Ltd.

Recommended Reading

Ackroyd, J., Neelands, J. *et al.* (1999) *Key Shakespeare 1: English and Drama Activities for Teaching Shakespeare to 10 – 14 Year Olds.* London: Hodder & Stoughton.

Ackroyd, J. (2000) *Literacy Alive.* London: Hodder & Stoughton.

Clipson-Boyles, S. (1999) *Drama in the Primary Classroom.* London: David Fulton Publishers.

Fleming, M. (1996) *Starting Drama Teaching.* London: David Fulton Publishers.

Morgan, N. and Saxton, J. (1987) *Teaching Drama: A Mind of Many Wonders.* London: Hutchinson.

Neelands, J. (1992) *Learning Through Imagined Experience.* London: Hodder & Stoughton.

Neelands, J. and Goode, T. (2000) *Structuring Drama Work.* Cambridge: Cambridge University Press.

O'Neill, C. (1995) *Drama Worlds.* London: Heinemann.

Redman, G. and Lamont, G. (1994) *Drama – A Handbook for Primary Teachers.* London: BBC Education.

Winston, J. and Tandy, M. (2000) *Beginning Drama 4–11.* (2nd edn). London: David Fulton Publishers.

Woolland, B. (1993) *The Teaching of Drama in the Primary School.* London: Longman.

Index